Game Devs and Others

Tales from the Margins

Game Devs and Others
Tales from the Margins

Edited by
Tanya DePass

CRC Press
Taylor & Francis Group
Boca Raton London New York

CRC Press is an imprint of the
Taylor & Francis Group, an **informa** business

CRC Press
Taylor & Francis Group
6000 Broken Sound Parkway NW, Suite 300
Boca Raton, FL 33487-2742

International Standard Book Number-13: 978-1-1385-5904-2 (Hardback)
                                        978-1-1385-5901-1 (Paperback)

Library of Congress Cataloging-in-Publication Data

Names: DePass, Tanya, author.
Title: Game devs & others : tales from the margins / Tanya DePass.
Other titles: Game devs and others
Description: Boca Raton, FL : CRC Press, 2018. | Includes index.
Identifiers: LCCN 2018002865| ISBN 9781138559011 (pbk. : alk. paper) | ISBN 9781138559042 (hardback : alk. paper)
Subjects: LCSH: Video games industry. | Internet games industry. | Minorities in technology. | Women in technology.
Classification: LCC HD9993.E452 D47 2018 | DDC 794.8092/2--dc23
LC record available at https://lccn.loc.gov/2018002865

**Visit the Taylor & Francis Web site at
http://www.taylorandfrancis.com**

**and the CRC Press Web site at
http://www.crcpress.com**

This book is dedicated to every person of color, LGBTQIA person, agender, and gender nonconforming person who is part of the gaming industry, past, present, and future. It's dedicated to everyone who fights, who left and returned, or was pushed out by hate. It's for everyone who wants to enter this world with the hope of more people like them both on screen and behind the scenes. It's for everyone who wants to hit start and know that the character who looks and sounds like them was crafted by people who care, who get it, and who want there to be more options than the assumed default.

Contents

Acknowledgments

THIS BOOK COULD NOT have happened without Jennifer Hepler and the trust she showed in asking me to take on this anthology. It's been such a ride from the initial conversation, to running around in my living room and flailing in joy, panic, happiness, and, let's be honest, fear that I'd massively screw all this up somehow. I mean, this is the creator of my favorite game of all time who reached out to ask me to edit this anthology. It's humbling and an honor to have done this.

Thank you to everyone who submitted an essay and shared their stories, whether they were chosen or not for this book. It took courage to share, and I thank you all for opening yourselves up to a review of such personal tales.

Special thanks go to NK Jemisin, a beloved friend and mentor and someone who inspires me, whether she knows it or not. Much thanks go to Tiffany Murphy, who really kept me going this past year, through all the times I wanted to quit doing I Need Diverse Games because it seemed untenable or not worth it after a hard day or week.

Love to the LHSYEA, who gave a lot of love, laughs, and shenanigans during multiplayer sessions after a long day of emails, editing, and such. To Manveer Heir, whose 2014 GDC talk lit a fire under me and is one I revisit for inspiration. To the board of I Need Diverse Games who supported this project—and me as I wrangled a lot of words to make it this book that wound up in your hands.

Thanks to Michi Trota, who supported me when I sent those what am I doing, why did I think I could pull this off?! Panicked GChat messages at random hours when I felt like an utter failure and fraud during this process. Also Christina Riser, who has been my fancy drink supplier and supporter from their spot far away from where I reside. Your support has helped so much, Socks.

To everyone who's supported me in word, deed, money, or time. There are too many to list in such a small space, but you, too, made this possible. No work is ever made by a single person, without support and encouragement from others. Thank you all.

Last but definitely not least, Sean Connelly and the folks at CRC Press supported and helped me and answered all emails from a newcomer to this part of publishing sent at oh-my-dog-why-do-you-have-so-many-question-this-early. Thank you for your patience and for giving me a chance along with Jennifer to bring these stories to you, reader.

Editor

Tanya DePass is the founder and director of I Need Diverse Games, a nonprofit organization based in Chicago dedicated to better diversification of all aspects of gaming. I Need Diverse Games serves the community by supporting marginalized developers in attending the Game Developers Conference (GDC) by participating in the GDC Scholarship program, helps assist attendance at other industry events, and seeks partnership with organizations and initiatives.

Tanya is a lifelong Chicagoan who loves everything about gaming and the originator of the #INeedDiverseGames hashtag, born of frustration with the gaming climate of 2014. She wants to make the industry better and more inclusive for everyone. She founded and was the Editor in Chief of Fresh Out of Tokens podcast, where games culture was discussed and viewed through a lens of feminism, intersectionality, and diversity. Now she's a cohost on the Spawn on Me podcast. Along with all of that, she's the Programming Coordinator for OrcaCon, and often speaks on issues of diversity, feminism, race, intersectionality, and other topics at multiple conventions throughout the year. Her writing on games, as well as her critique of the medium, appears in *Uncanny Magazine*, *Polygon*, *WisCon Chronicles*, *Vice Gaming*, *Paste Games*, *Waypoint*, *Mic*, and other publications.

When Tanya isn't herding cats, reviewing GDC scholarship applications, or braving the winter temps of her hometown, she can be found sharing gaming and some creative endeavors on Twitch. Otherwise, she spends far too much time on Twitter as @cypheroftyr.

Contributors

Michael Annetta is a producer and designer based in Los Angeles. He has worked with, among others, MatterVR, Flying Mollusk, WEVR, and Walt Disney Imagineering. He has presented on games, transmedia, and virtual reality at PAX Prime, San Diego Comic-Con, Storyworld, NAMLE (National Association for Media Literacy Education), VR Long Beach, and Bent-Con.

Michael holds an MFA from the University of Southern California's (USC's) Interactive Media & Games division (where he was the first-ever recipient of the USC Lambda LGBT [lesbian, gay, bisexual, and transgender] Alumni Association's NOGLSTP [National Organization of Gay and Lesbian Scientists and Technical Professionals] Scholarship in Innovation). He currently teaches in the department as an adjunct professor.

Michael shifted into games after a long and diverse career as a performer, singer, director, and producer for stage and film. He has worked extensively in New York City, Chicago, and Los Angeles. When prompted, he can (and will) still perform a Shakespearean monologue or 16 bars of a ballad and uptempo.

Joshua Kyle Boykin is the founder and editor-in-chief of Intelligame.us, a website focusing on game culture, criticism, and community. With a deep love for storytelling and narratives, he focuses on finding intersections between games and reality, and showcasing those to others. He also loves creating community for gamers in real life, and is the organizer for TwitchPDX, a video game-centric group in Portland, OR. He can be found on Twitter at @Wallstormer.

Maurice Broaddus a community organizer and teacher, his work has appeared in *Lightspeed Magazine, Weird Tales, Apex Magazine*, Asimov's, *Cemetery Dance, Black Static*, and many more. Some of his stories have been collected in *The Voices of Martyrs*. He wrote the urban fantasy trilogy, *The Knights of Breton Court*. He coauthored the play, *Finding Home: Indiana* at 200. His novellas include *Buffalo Soldier*, *I Can Transform You*, *Orgy of Souls*, *Bleed with Me*, and *Devil's Marionette*. He is the coeditor of *Dark Faith*, *Dark Faith: Invocations*, *Streets of Shadows*, and *People of Colo(u)r Destroy Horror*. Learn more about him at MauriceBroaddus.com.

Shana T Bryant is a producer and a Level-15 industry veteran, who has successfully completed the Capcom, Midway Games, and Electronic Arts quests. She has had a hand in crafting some of your favorite games in the *Devil May Cry* and *Resident Evil* series (and might've even canceled a few). She's brought her depth of expertise from console to PC to AR/MR experiences and mobile. Shana is currently producing a new round of amazing not-yet-announced coolness at Take-Two Interactive in Seattle.

Shana speaks openly about her experiences as a woman of color in the games industry. In addition to contributing to the 2016 academic publication *Diversifying Barbie and Mortal Kombat*, Shana led workshops on designing inclusive interactions for emerging tech at 2016's Grace Hopper Conference and was an invited speaker in 2017 at the IGDA Next Generation Leaders Summit on the topic of career management for underrepresented professionals.

Shana is a passionate advocate of diversity and inclusion and is always open to a candid conversation, whether in a coffee shop or over some boardgames. She is an avid comic artist, expounding on ideas with spoonful of southern charm and just a touch of pith and snark.

For a deeper look at what makes Shana tick, check out her blog at the MushroomQueendom.com and her comic at terribleallies.com.

Alex Zandra Van Chestein has been a game designer, writer, and artist for the past 20 years. Having returned to independent work after years at a large studio, she now creates prototypes and games, streams speedruns and game analysis, draws adorable things, and—due to a strange series of events—now writes and illustrates light novels. She also organizes the Giant Bomb community game jam and is currently developing *One Last Cup*, a cyberpunk coffee shop conversation game.

Lauren Ashlee Comp is a game developer with a passion for romance in games. Hailing from southeast Michigan and currently residing in northern California, she works as junior producer leading a small team and directing narratives at Voltage Entertainment USA Inc. on Lovestruck.

Kadeem Dunn is a Mississauga-based video game curator, educator, and creator. Having worked with Hand Eye Society, Mississauga Culture, and in game education, Kadeem has contributed to the growing game culture of the Greater Toronto Area.

Toiya Kristen Finley is a writer, editor, game designer, and narrative designer/game writer. She holds a PhD in literature and creative writing from Binghamton University. With nearly 70 published works, she has 20 years of experience writing in a range of genres, tones, styles, and voices. In 2011, she co-founded the Game Writing Tutorial at GDC Online with Tobias Heussner and served as an instructor in 2011 and 2012. In videogames, she has worked as a game designer, narrative designer, game writer, and editor (or some combination of the four) on several unreleased and in-production indie, social, and mobile games for children and general audiences. Some of these projects shall stay locked away in dungeons for eternity (hey, that's the game industry for ya). Some published games include *Academagia: The Making of Mages* (Black Chicken Studios), *Fat Chicken* (Relevant Games), and *Peregrin* (Domino Digital Limited). She coauthored *The Game Narrative Toolbox* (Focal Press, 2015), a book on narrative design, with Jennifer Brandes Hepler, Ann Lemay, and Tobias Heussner. She is a member of the IGDA (International Game Developers Association) Game Writing Special Interest Group's Executive Board. Her current projects include *Narrative Tactics for Mobile and Social Games: Pocket-Sized Storytelling* (CRC Press, 2018) and narrative design and game design on projects for a VR start-up.

Jaym Gates is an editor, author, and project manager based in Seattle, WA. She has edited titles including *Broken Time Blues*, *Upside Down*, *Strange California*, *Legends of Strategy*, *Eclipse Phase: After the Fall*, *Genius Loci*, and *War Stories*. Her fiction has appeared in Goldfish Grimm, Grendelsong, M-Brane SF, and many more, as well as in her short story collection, Shattered Queen. She acquires and develops fiction for Falstaff Books and other clients. She is the line manager for Nisaba Press, and Green Ronin's editorial coordinator. You can find out more about her at jaymgates.com, or on Twitter as @JaymGates.

KN Granger is a queer cisgender white queer woman who lives in New York City. Titles of note include *Ghost Ship Enyo*, an out-loud text adventure game, *Advocating Creatively*, an anthology of social justice artists, *A Trip to Dr. Fielgude*, a game about mental health and aging. She also has written or co-written around a dozen chamber Live Action Roleplaying Games, and she also actively writes fanfiction and other stories. Her website can be viewed at roseclue.com and she also is accessible on Twitter under the handle @RoseClue.

Shareef Jackson has been obsessed with technology ever since he was a child, disassembling remote controls and driving his parents crazy. As the founder of the math and physics tutoring service *Math Looks Good LLC*, Shareef's culturally relevant communication style helps break down science, gaming, and math in a way that the average person can understand and appreciate. His views on science and technology have been featured on sources such as the *New York Times*, *National Public Radio*, *Scientific American*, and *MacLean's*. Shareef is a co-host on the Spawn on Me podcast, which spotlights people of color in gaming. He highlights issues of gender and race on his YouTube series at Gaming Looks Good.

He has attended several events including the final launch of NASA's space shuttle program, the International Society for Technology in Education (ITSE), Consumer Electronics Show (CES), the Game Developers Conference (GDC), and the Electronics Entertainment Expo (E3).

Jonathan Jennings had the pleasure of working on over a dozen games and apps available to the public, his work has seen over 2 million combined downloads. Currently he is exploring the brave new world of AR/VR and is always excited to see, learn, and explore what's next on the technical horizon.

Kat Jones is a queer, Latina game designer, organizer, and scholar. She has extensive experience with research and teaching in the fields of sociology as well as women, gender, and sexuality studies. Jones has written and coauthored a wide range of live-action scenarios, including *Glitzy Nails* in #Feminism, Revived: A Support Group for the Partially Deceased, and her entry to the Queer Gaymes anthology, Glitter Pits, which was awarded Best Intersectional Game Involving Experiences of Queer People of Color. Jones has helped organize several live-action events at community art spaces and has run her games at conferences and conventions including GenCon, QGCon, and Origins. She was recently on the organizing teams for the U.S. run of Just a Little Lovin' and the initial run of Immerton.

Elizabeth LaPensée, PhD is an award-winning writer, designer, and artist of games, comics, and animation. She is Anishinaabe, Métis, and Irish, living near the Great Lakes as an assistant professor of Media & Information and Writing, Rhetoric & American Cultures at Michigan State University. She designed and created art for *Thunderbird Strike* (2017), a side-scrolling lightning-searing attack on oil operations.

JC Lau works in test at Bungie and is a member of the studio's Diversity Committee. Prior to entering the games industry, she was professor in the philosophy of race and gender at Virginia Tech, having earned her doctorate in political philosophy from the Australian National University in 2012. She has spoken on race and gender at PAX, Emerald City Comicon, and GeekGirlCon, and has been featured on several podcasts at the intersection of gaming and representation.

Hadeel al-Massari is an Arab-American writer, coder, and independent business owner based in Seattle, WA. She is a D.Va main in *Overwatch*, falls off a lot of cliffs in *Breath of the Wild*, and loves running errands for her villagers in *Animal Crossing*. She's worked at Nintendo, freelanced with several indie companies, and now works at a financial tech company. She may or may not have an obsession with knitting socks.

Scout Munroe is a game tester, YouTuber, aspiring voice actor, and longtime lover of games located in San Diego. In their spare time, they enjoy good food, interesting convention panels, and can be found just about everywhere on the Internet as 'ThisisMunroe.'

Vanessa Paugh as chief visioneer of Goddess Software since 2003, Vanessa Paugh utilized her many years of software development experience to create the *I am the Bride* Flash game series. Her academic achievements include a PhD in aesthetic studies, an MFA in arts and technology, an MS in engineering and a BEE in electrical engineering. Dr. Paugh started shipping iOS games to the App Store in 2009, including *iGown*, *Pride And Prejudice RPG* and *Closets And Connections*. She is currently working on a new game in Unity3D.

Matthue Roth is the author of the picture book *The Gobblings* and some other books without pictures. He helped create the Google Assistant, has been a screenwriter for Sesame Street, and coedits the website Hevria. He also keeps a secret diary at matthue.com.

Dorey T Shawn grew up in the one true city of New Brunswick, Moncton. He was raised on city-tempered rural hegemonic masculinity that was heightened by geek culture. After tumbling around computer science and business degrees at the University of New Brunswick, Shawn got woke on feminism and media analysis in UNB's Media Arts and Cultures program.

After finishing his honor's degree in media arts and cultures, he studied video games and culture in the University of Waterloo's English Department while examining his gender and biracial (Arab{Lebanese}/White) privilege and heritage through poetry. His favorite video game is *Kingdom Hearts*. Catch Shawn on Twitter as @ShawnDorey.

Steven Spohn is the chief operations officer and community outreach director for AbleGamers charity, award-winning author, and advocate for people with disabilities. Featured on CNN, NBC, and other mainstream news outlets as an assistive technology and game accessibility expert, Steven brings all his knowledge and much more to champion for people with disabilities in the video game space as a means of defeating social isolation. Steve has also traveled the country speaking at various prestigious events. When not writing or doing charity work, you can find him gaming, reading the latest sci-fi novels, or cracking jokes on social media—@StevenSpohn or Facebook.com/StevenSpohn. He currently resides outside of Pittsburgh, Pennsylvania with his adorable ragdoll cat and sheltie puppy.

Kaitlin Tremblay is a narrative designer at Ubisoft and a writer. She is the author of the book *Ain't No Place for a Hero: Borderlands* (ECW Press, 2017), and the coeditor of the Shirley Jackson Award-nominated anthology *Those Who Make Us: Canadian Creature, Myth, and Monster Stories* (Exile Editions, 2016). Tremblay was the lead writer on the IGF (Independent Games Festival) award-nominated death positive game *A Mortician's Tale* (Laundry Bear, 2017).

Introduction

THIS PROJECT HAS BEEN an honor to work on, and it's been a little frightening to take on such a task from someone I regard so highly. It's also been an immense pleasure to have people trust me with their personal tales of their time in the industry, as well as to hear stories from those who are on the edges of it. It was quite the learning experience as I went through this process as an editor instead of someone sending their words out for consideration and review.

I gave a lot of thanks in the acknowledgements section, but there are always more to give, since this project could not have happened without the work of many. Thanks to Jennifer Hepler for reaching out and asking if I'd do this. Thanks to everyone who submitted an essay that didn't make it into the final volume: your stories are important, and I hope you get to share them.

Thank you to Tiffany Murphy for helping me review when I'd hit that point of being unable to read anything else for fear of overthinking and overanalyzing the text. Also for being a rock in rough seas of self-doubt.

CHAPTER 1

Fight-Free Fashion Agency

Vanessa Paugh

I N LINE WITH THE definition of marginalized game developer, I am invisible to the press and the consciousness of the game industry. However, I do exist and have been on the fringes of the industry for thirteen years. Like most game developers, I started making games because I enjoyed playing some of them, but I couldn't find "the perfect game." I wanted to find a game that didn't force me to fight and that did allow me to carry my real-life fashion sense into the game. I didn't realize it at first, but I also wanted to have direct control over my character's movement. It seems like a small thing, but it is rare to find games with female player characters who have been programmed to allow this.

Looking deeper, I found that the search for a fight-free environment, where I could wear what I wanted and take action, had come from my real life. Being Black, my every move was literally being policed, and being female, my fashion choices were being curtailed. Fortunately, the act of game development increases agency, in games and in real life. For me, that feeling of making textured hair and beautiful clothes for game characters, while wearing natural hair and comfortable clothes, is like no other agency. I've learned how to make games as an independent developer, to eliminate the fighting, in game and out of game. My biggest frustration is the depth of war orientation in the language of the pedagogy. Right now, it is impossible to learn game development without confronting guns and explosions. My hope is that people like me can show that it doesn't have to be that way.

Ruth Handler must have had girls like me in mind when she created Barbie. I loved paper dolls so much, I made my own. A 3D version of a fashion paper doll was right up my alley. You can imagine how I felt when Mattel announced *Barbie Fashion Designer* (BFD), the computer game. It was only available on PC and I only had a Mac, but I bought a copy of the game anyway. My then boyfriend, now husband, graciously allowed me to install it, albeit temporarily, on his PC. I delighted in gaining the ability to design virtual and real clothes for Barbie. The 3D fashion show capability was amazing.

By the time BFD came out, an idea I had for a closet organizer, with a similar paper-doll-style interface, had already been rejected by two thesis advisors as not technical enough. Undeterred, I built it in a graduate-level object-oriented programming class. However, I thought of it as a tool, not a game. I thought of myself as a developer, not a game developer.

Later, when the Mac version of BFD arrived, I bought it also. Having the ability to make virtual clothes at any time made me perfectly happy. I didn't want anything more from BFD than more of what it already was. Barbie can never have enough different styles of clothes. I didn't notice that anything was missing when Barbie walked down the runway, without my control. I didn't know anything about the concepts of player and player character, versus nonplayer character. The idea that Barbie was the in-game model and that I was the out-of-game designer was enough for me.

I played every dress-up computer game and, later, online game I could find. Learning how to make them was my gateway to other languages, such as HTML, ActionScript, Java, Javascript, Objective-C, and C#, and tools, such as Hypercard, Director, Flash, Xcode, and Unity. They were my first step into new technology, and they always had the same elements. There was a flat, immobile figure with many, many different outfit variations. She generally couldn't move her arms or legs, and she couldn't walk or wear her clothes to places outside the design studio. She was literally all dressed up with nowhere to go.

Alternatively, the locomotion controls in *Tomb Raider* were revolutionary at the time. The transfer from real-life hand movement to avatar movement was so fluid that I really felt like I was Lara Croft and Lara Croft was me. Lara's world was so vivid and she (I) was so much the mistress of it that I knew agency and couldn't go back. I played *Tomb Raider* to the point of dysphoria when I hit pause. My ordinary suburban house seemed out of place next to the predator-filled cabin I had just experienced.

Lara was so much an extension of me that wearing the same clothes level after level started to bother me. First, it was the monotony, then it occurred to me that I would have never chosen those drab khaki shorts. I remembered that I had worn a black racerback top and sweatpants during the training level, so I tried to get them into the game, to no avail. Even the ponytail started to get old, since its color wasn't one I would have chosen. That ponytail didn't have my own hair color or texture. Finally, when I noticed that her skin color wasn't pivotal to the story, but couldn't be changed to match mine, I contemplated stopping. My frustration grew, but I decided to keep playing because the game got better and my fusion with the Lara avatar grew stronger. I realized that I had taken a step forward in agency, only to be forced backward in personalization, because I couldn't take this step as myself.

If all the levels in *Tomb Raider* had been only mildly interesting, and not breathtakingly beautiful, I would have continued to be a gamer and a developer, but I would never have become a game dev. It's sad that the inability to be myself did not stop me from playing that game. It took a dinosaur biting my head off to do that. It wasn't the dying that did it. I died hundreds of times in that game and just reloaded my last saved game to keep playing.

It was deep in level 15 or so that the gray caverns gave way to the most luscious green-leaved trees in an underground jungle. I was overcome with the desire to stop and smell the… That was when the dinosaur got me. I had forgotten that I was in a life-threatening game. After reloading the level and killing the dinosaurs back into extinction, I just walked around and allowed the beauty to wash over me. The fact that people had put so much effort into making each leaf look so realistic flashed through my mind.

That's when it hit me: I shouldn't have to kill everything to see something so beautiful. There could be so many interesting and glamourous places recreated in a game world that would be ruined by having to have a battle first to experience them. Instead of predators, there could be friendly people who would ask me to tea. That was the moment when I became a game developer, even though I didn't realize it at the time. In my mind, I could see a game that didn't exist—and that wouldn't if the same people kept making the same kind of games. To get to the peaceful virtual place where I could wear my own skin, hair, and clothes while directly controlling my avatar's arms and legs, I was going to have to up my game dev skills and make it myself.

This quest for fight-free, fashion-filled agency in a game mirrors my real-life struggle. After I had shipped a couple of games with brown-skinned protagonists, a well-meaning white friend asked why I was limiting my market share. No one asks why a company with only white male protagonist games is limiting its market share. Everyone just assumes that females and males of color will play their games, if they are good. My friend didn't tell me to make sure my game was good so males and white females would play it. He, and many others, just assumed that they wouldn't play it. Quality is irrelevant when the protagonist doesn't look like my white male friend.

This argument is still being used to keep the default game protagonists white and male, which keeps the default writers, artists, and developers white and male as well. When the game company's core team is white and male, they decide that the default player is white and male, which justifies making the default protagonist white and male. The circle of white males is formed. There is no place for people who look like me to move into. We lose our agency at every level in the game and the industry. They don't see us in the meeting, so they can't see us playing the game, so we don't end up in the game. We become those flat, immobile figures who they dress up in the nongamer stereotype and give no place to go.

To resist, I don't play fighting games, for the most part. I steel myself, if I need to do it to learn something. The first thing I do in a tutorial is change the race and gender of the protagonist. This has led to some interesting mods where I, a black female with a weapon, am chasing down white males and killing them.

I don't show them at game dev meetups, but I have been to a few. Before going to my first one, I agonized over my attire. I chose red high-top converse, black menswear jeans, and a plain red T-shirt with an open red and black plaid shirt over it. It turned out that I had on the same shoes as one of the organizers and I looked like I belonged. However, that isn't how I normally dress, and I didn't feel comfortable at all. The second time, I felt comfortable wearing teal and blue weaved crock sandals, teal earrings, a gray and white striped maxi skirt, and a white jewel neck knit blouse with a gray and white sweater over it. Needless to say, I didn't match anyone, and I didn't look like I belonged in that room full of white men. I just want to hang out with other game developers and not feel like I have to wear someone else's clothes.

When I'm working, I wear whatever I want, because I work from home. If I need to know something, I read a book or find an online tutorial. Although I took several college classes in programming, 3D modeling, and *Photoshop*, I only took one university course in actual game design. When the professor of that class announced that feminism was dead, I did wish it had been a video, so I could have just turned her off. To be fair, it was in context. On the other hand, she and I were the only women in a room full of twenty-something white males. As much as I hate fighting, I chose to fight in that instance. I said that feminism is still alive because we still don't have equal pay for equal work. I didn't back down because that is the only class I have ever been in where "feminism is dead" has been proclaimed. If I hadn't been in that class, no one would have pushed back. Perhaps, dead feminism would have become part of the curriculum. Game design pedagogy is problematic enough without generations of new male designers being told to keep using that woman-in-refrigerator trope because women don't care about equality anymore.

While I learned most of what I know about game design from that professor, she, like many women in the industry, have adopted the game = war mentality from the men. She critiqued the game that I made for my master's capstone project and asked about the main gameplay mechanic. I told her it would be designing clothes and dressing models. She said it wouldn't really be a game. I said there could be a game with no fighting. She asked what you would do in it otherwise. This is true to the nature of the industry. At a game meetup, a gamer expressed a similar sentiment—that without fighting, it isn't really a game.

This perspective is so deeply ingrained in game playing and game development culture that it is impossible to even learn to make games without confronting virtual weapons. This was a huge turn-off for me, as it is for many women and some men who don't want to make war games. I've learned to keep my ideas and designs to myself during the incubation period of a game project. People will tell me that something isn't a game or can't be done, when I'm unsure. The best solution is to try it and build the prototype, which eliminates the "can't be done" argument. Then it doesn't matter whether or not someone else calls it a game; it's out there in the store.

During my dev retreat, I cherish the moments when I imagine some female's face smiling in delight as she finds her skin tone among the choices. I remember playing a game where anything but blonde hair cost game currency. I do the tedious job of adding one more texture to the hair pack while my favorite songs play. I remember when a game company gave players a choice of three male protagonists, but said that having one female playable character was too much work. I get high on my code running the first time after a slew of changes. I remember when the Internet lost its mind because players had to play as randomly chosen female characters. I feel so happy when my virtual clothes fit and look cute on. I remember all the times I had to code-switch my language when talking or when I understood something when trying to apply what I'd learned. I wake up in the morning, and I can't wait to get to work on the next piece of the puzzle.

Although I thought my work was done when *The Sims* came out, it taught me the difference between direct agency and indirect autonomy. As designed, the main gameplay mechanic of the game is not fighting. Sims can be customized and personalized. Sims can move and walk, and the real player can tell them what to do. However, the actions are indirect, and so is the connection. I view sims like minions versus extensions of my real self.

Since I still haven't found everything I want in a game, I keep trying to learn more about game development, modeling, and storytelling. I will keep making games until I realize my vision of the perfect game. It will feature zero fighting, fashion flexibility, and all agency, all the time.

CHAPTER 2

Alex Zandra Van Chestein

I GOT MY FIRST JOB in the industry just before turning 30, after years of making freeware indie games by myself. It was my dream job, in the very homogenous sleepy-big-town of Quebec City. For five years I worked at a large studio on a ton of different projects, having the time of my life. One such project sent me to PAX to help with the booth, where I truly discovered Seattle, the game dev community at large, and so many wonderful queer folks. And that's when I finally accepted I was trans. Six months later, I came out.

I was already known as one of the most positive people in the company; I was easily excited, I joked often, I was the first to volunteer for talks and presentations, and I had done my best to be everyone's friend. So when everyone got the news, they welcomed me with open arms.

I was the first trans person most of the 350 people working at the company had ever met, and the first to transition while working there.

The first few days were exhilarating; I had been in denial for more than 15 years, and ever being able to be myself was a dream I'd long since given up on. I was discovering how to be me, figuring out who I was, and learning a lot all at once. I also had to do a lot of educating; some of my coworkers who hadn't gotten the news burst out laughing when they saw me walk into the office while presenting as a woman. I was selected to be in the company newsletter as that month's interviewee, but instead of talking about me and my work, I gave everyone the transgender 101 basics to help them understand where I was coming from.

Uniformly, the women I worked with were wonderful and supportive, but that was true only for some of the men. Those I'd worked with before tended to be more receptive and quick to adapt, while others continued to misgender me for months. The place where I would always get 100% safety and support was the ladies' room; I still remember clear as day the time I was fussing with my wig in the mirror and a coworker walked by and cheerfully reassured me, saying I was beautiful. It helped so much.

(During the first month, HR told me that some of my coworkers were uncomfortable with me going into the women's bathroom and asked me to go to the unisex single-user bathroom on a different floor. But they never brought it up again, and the constant positive reinforcement I got from the women working with me encouraged me to keep using the facilities on my floor.)

Getting to be myself was a wonderful experience, but I soon discovered—as every femme-presenting person does—what sexism was firsthand. The silver lining was, of course, that I was being treated as a woman, and that was nice; but work soon became so much more than I could handle. I had heard stories from my friends, and I did my best to prepare myself, but it still took so much out of me.

Male coworkers who hadn't known me before were skeptical of my game development skills; I was a game designer, after all, not a programmer, so who had made those games for me? (I had.) In meetings, my ideas were constantly shot down and passed over in favor of others'. Colleagues lectured me on how I should be designing with an audience in mind, as if I hadn't already been doing that for over five years alongside them. My supervisor, with whom I previously got along well, started having daily team checkup meetings without me; he'd sit down with the programmers and talk, leaving me the task of figuring out when it was happening and tracking them down. He was bewildered to hear that this made me feel excluded.

The pattern of exclusion was immensely more noticeable now that I was—openly—the only woman in a team of 20+ designers. The company had hired women for game design positions in the past, but it had never succeeded in keeping them; they invariably left, to be replaced by another woman who would then stay about a year or two before also heading off. I had remained undetected as a woman all this time, helped into the professional side of the industry by mentors and no doubt a significant amount of privilege.

Colleagues had trouble adjusting their speech in meetings and brainstorms, always addressing the room as if there were no women present (even in French, the "guys-is-gender-neutral" phenomenon is alive and well). Even after being asked repeatedly to be more inclusive in their language, my coworkers resisted. Those microaggressions, added to the difficulty of being heard in group discussions, made meetings go from one of my favorite work-related activities to something I no longer wanted a part in. I'll always remember the one moment I spectacularly made myself heard during a brainstorm session where someone cut me off, misinterpreted what I had said, and proceeded to begin a long-winded explanation as to why I was wrong. I literally shouted him down. It's surprising just how taken aback people are when you yell "HEY!" in a meeting room, then proceed to calmly explain the misunderstanding and your annoyance at being interrupted. The incident was thoroughly discussed during my subsequent performance review, but it did not diminish how glad I was to have stood up for myself.

This wasn't to be the only time I'd have a talk about my behavior at work. While I had previously been working towards inclusivity and representation in our games, no one really took notice until I came out—and then suddenly I met more resistance. Some people were sympathetic to my cause in the design department, but progress was still difficult to achieve. I recall a heated discussion with my supervisor, where he maintained that it was impossible to make humor that didn't offend anyone and that it was a necessary evil when joking. The numerous examples of other game companies doing just that—humor that is not at the expense of anyone— couldn't sway his mind. It did, however, prompt him to have a meeting with me and an HR representative about my work ethic.

The HR rep called my supervisor and me into a small meeting room, where I was told that they had noticed I'd been very vocal about making our games more inclusive and diverse, but this was making my colleagues uncomfortable, so I needed to stop doing that. Going into damage control, I was too stunned to speak my mind; I wanted to get out of that room with my job intact. So I nodded. And then—likely because of the conversation I mentioned earlier—they asked me to confirm that, if asked to, I would work on a project that had offensive humor in it. I said what I needed to say to get out of the room, but that short, three-person meeting was the moment I realized I needed to leave that town.

I had done my best to educate and spread the word and fight for a better culture, but I couldn't take it much longer. In my own self-interest, I had to move away. I started looking into travel and immigration; I looked into the feasibility of certain plans. I was going west; luck would determine how far I'd end up. In the meantime, I continued my work, but I was less socially involved, less vocal about my opinions; the meeting had had the intended effect.

I lasted two more months.

Come the end of January, I was drained and pushed to my limits by the deteriorating environment and microaggressions. Every meeting became a fight, and I was getting so exhausted by having to spend so much energy to make just a little headway. When another supervisor called me into his office, I fully assumed it was about my recent performance; I assumed everyone could tell I was doing terrible work and getting nothing done. But instead, he was concerned; he'd burned out before and was worried I was headed in that direction myself.

I took his advice and went to the local clinic to talk to a doctor. I told her about the potential burnout and she gave me a questionnaire to fill out. I almost got a maximum score, sobbing by the time I reached the last question. I went back to work to pack up my things and let them know I'd be on medical leave for two months. I had no idea things had gotten this bad.

It took me weeks to relearn how to relax. I was so on edge, so constantly ready to have to defend myself, that I'd completely lost the ability to take care of myself. I needed every single day of that leave; I'd never realized what burnout truly was, or how long it took to heal from it, if at all. It would take me more than a year to get back to a place where I was able to work again.

I went on trips, I saw friends, I talked about my personal projects, I became a little bit more of a person day by day. I healed. And when it came time to renew my lease, I didn't. I'd made my choice; I was going to Montreal. It wasn't as far as the west coast, but it was full of people I cared about, it made travel easier, and the indie game community was stronger. And, more importantly, its culture was a lot friendlier to me from the get-go.

When my medical leave ended, so did my employment. I went home, prepared to move, and did some part-time design work at a small studio for a few months before having to quit. I still wasn't ready for full-time work then, even if the tiny team I was working with was leagues ahead of anything else I'd ever known. That was my last job.

It's been more than a year since I burned out, moved away, and slowly recovered. I've found my ideal way to work: freelance, for myself, in collaboration with others sometimes, but mostly by creating things and fostering a following. I've gotten involved in the local communities, I've spread my wings artistically, I've done things I never would've dreamed myself capable of before. I used to strive for security and stability, but now I've discovered how important freedom can be, even if it's so financially precarious.

I'm still making games; I'm also writing, and making art, and streaming, and presenting talks, and doing anything and everything I can in the games industry and beyond. But it's going to take a while—or a very special opportunity—for me to go back to a 9-to-5 job again. When you work for yourself, you don't get misgendered or belittled by your coworkers. You don't get uplifted as much, but I've been working on that.

Working with local communities has helped on that front, too. I've sometimes overcommitted how much energy I could put into it, but being a part, however small, of organizations that help marginalized folks get into games, that help independent artists and creators get much-needed attention, has been incredibly fulfilling. It's amazing the difference it makes to have friends on your side, to have a support network; I don't think I could live without it now.

A year or so ago, someone asked me in an interview why I made games, and my answer still hasn't changed: I want to change the world. I want to make games for people who don't have many opportunities to see themselves in games; I want to set better examples. I want to contribute to the games culture I want to see in the world. And if I need to be especially careful about where I work to accomplish that, then that's fine with me.

I'm sad I couldn't stay in Quebec City and help change the culture there for the better, but I've been trying to accept that. I did the best I could under the circumstances. Ultimately, I moved to a place where I could take care of myself better. Transitioning has been the best decision of my life; despite it all, I'd do it again in a heartbeat. I'm finally proud of who I am, and I know I have the support of so many wonderful people. I want to do my best to be a positive influence on the culture, on others, and on the world at large— even if just a tiny little bit.

Let's keep making wonderful things together.

CHAPTER 3

Resistance and Survival Through Community and Horror

Kaitlin Tremblay

Content warning: This essay includes a significant amount of discussion on trauma recovery, eating disorders, and self-harm.

THE THING ABOUT EATING disorders is that they're so often about control. Not always, of course, but often enough it's a sort of cliché to say. Gaining control. Claiming some sort of power over a chemical, mental, and physical whirlwind of pain, anger, fear, and confusion. Taking charge in the face of feeling helpless. This sounds heroic because we're taught that being in control is. But it's not when what's sacrificed as the cost of this control is far greater, of course. Mental illness isn't rational; it's chemical.

Creating games—small, personal, body horror games—about what it's like to navigate the murky and confusing realm of mental illness and trauma recovery is a form of taking back control. It's a way of exercising ownership over my mental illness while also speaking honestly about my experiences in trying and build bridges to others.

Rather than a control over my body, making games is a control over my story, a way of forcing people to listen. Mental health activism, particularly that centered around eating disorders, tends to erase people's lived experiences in lieu of focusing solely on how their bodies present, rather than what they feel and undergo. The conversation always seems to stop at appearance. We only acknowledge what we see with eating disorders. We rarely look beyond appearance because we've been taught that it's a disorder only about appearances.

My body horror games about eating disorders are entirely text-based, in an effort to shift the focus from what bodies look *like* during eating disorders, in order to give myself the space necessary to talk about what eating disorders actually *feel* like. In my very first game, *Stop Me If You've Heard This One Before*, I made a conscious decision not to include any visual references to what Elizabeth, the playable character, looks like, because conversations about eating disorders always get derailed into fixating on what a body looks like rather than what that body is undergoing.

My games specifically use body horror to talk about mental illness through this lens to address the ways marginalized bodies and experiences are violently erased or talked about in many conversations about mental health—and about eating disorders specifically. Focusing on anorexic bodies erases people with bulimia, with binge-eating disorder, or with any other diagnosis that falls under the broad categorization of eating disorder. Focusing on only one specific body type in this conversation means the erasure of other body types and experiences, just as focusing on only women with eating disorders is an erasure of cis and trans men and people who are nonbinary or gender fluid. Nobody is immune to eating disorders.

In the 2017 Rue Morgue supplement, *Women with Guts: Horror Heroines in Film, TV, and Print*, author Alison Lang* explores the myriad of ways women have resisted, reclaimed, and become empowered through horror, from Ripley in *Alien* to the girl in *A Girl Walks Home Alone At Night*. In her article, "Horror Movies Are One of the Few Places Women Are Told Their Fears Are Real," Gita Jackson writes, "Here are the things I am afraid of. Now you know that they are real,"† nailing the idea that what makes horror appealing to women and marginalized folks is that it's the one place people are prepared to actually believe our fears when we talk about them.

Creating any art is empowerment. Creating horror games is a radical way of demanding to be believed. Horror can be mobilized as a feminist

---

* Lang, A. 2017. *Women with Guts: Horror Heroines in Film, TV, and Print*. Rue Morgue Library. https://rue-morgue.com/product/rue-morgue-library-10-women-with-guts/

† Jackson, G. 2015. *Horror Movies Are One of the Few Places Women Are Told Their Fears Are Real*. https://www.polygon.com/2015/4/29/8490019/horror-films-women

genre because it is the only genre in which not only are women's fears inherently believed, but to disbelieve, deride, and ignore women's fear results in a lot of bloodshed. It's validating. And the amount of people that respond to my body horror games about mental illness with sympathy and a hopeful but exhausted "I didn't know others felt this same way" is a testament to the power of this notion.

Stop Me If You've Heard This One Before is an ugly game. It's a text-based game with ugly color for the hyperlinks, on top of an ugly colored background, with a small, unreadable font. I knew nothing about CSS and programming at the time, but knew I wanted to—and needed to—tell this story. But its ugliness reflects back how I felt then, and it's something I no longer despise about the game. I was in an ugly state and I made an ugly game. And that's part of its power: I was able to make it and release it when I needed to, even if I didn't entirely know what I was doing.

This type of reclamation of voice and use of self-dismemberment as a metaphor was possible only through video games and the interactivity that video games afford. Having the player guide Elizabeth's hand, choosing which body part to dismember, was not a mindless choice: interactivity created a necessary sense of complicitness. The way eating disorder jokes are commonly accepted in mainstream media, the way fatphobia is not just accepted but also actively encouraged, is a societal problem, and implicating the player in Elizabeth's actions was a call for the players to consider their own complicitness in perpetuating the silence that surrounds and enables eating disorders.

But creating games instead of traditional fiction was more than just needing the interactivity of games to drive home certain points I wanted to make. It was about community and survival through that community. Eating disorders are intensely alienating—being around others tips them off to our eating habits, revealing the bits of disorder we require to function. So often people with disordered eating close off, shut out the world that threatens to crumble the disordered routine we've structured around ourselves like a safety net.

Community is the exact antithesis of this.

This need to heal through community prompted me to create a Twine anthology called *Lights Out, Please*, a collection of Twine games from diverse creators about daily fears. Its premise is people sitting around a campfire sharing urban legends and ghost stories. But these urban legends are all subverted to be about daily rituals, like going to the bathroom as a transwoman or about coping mechanics for surviving abuse from parents.

The idea originally came from a line in the 1990 documentary *Paris Is Burning*, where one of the drag queens says that riding the subway is the scariest part of the day. We know fear intimately as marginalized people.

Lights Out, Please didn't make a lot of money and it didn't get a lot of press coverage, but it brought together a small group of people that talked openly about their fears and gave them a space to share these fears with people who would nod, smile, and say, "I totally get this. You're not alone." Some wrote under pseudonyms to protect themselves but still remarked upon how good it felt to share with others and to be supported and believed.

At the most difficult juncture in my eating disorder recovery path I was enrolled in various group therapy programs. I was in a group specifically designed for trans and cis women and nonbinary folks to work through their eating disorder recovery by simultaneously working through trauma recovery. In this group I realized how important community and collaborative efforts were to my recovery. It wasn't about taking from others, it was about being vulnerable together, listening and supporting, and growing together through our awkward, unsure, and often differing paths of recovery. We fought, and we challenged one another, but we also supported each other, and listened, giving validation and empathy to emotions that were difficult to express. We dissented, we clashed, we laughed, and we smiled, but even when it was difficult, even when showing up took all of our energy, we weren't alone.

One night, after a particularly exhausting and emotionally intense session, one woman, who rarely spoke, said something I'll never forget: "It's nice just to be held by other women who get it, you know?"

My therapist, when I initially began getting help, told me that she would see me, but I also had to attend these group sessions on my own. I didn't get it at first. I was angry, I didn't want to spend more time than an hour a week thinking about this, digging up old trauma and leaving myself raw and exposed. But after that trauma group, I understood. After hearing that woman in my trauma group say that, I got it. There are some things we just can't do alone. In an aggressive world and industry, community is survival.

This space—game dev space—isn't necessarily feminist. But there are plenty of spaces within game development that are feminist, antiracist, and inclusive, where people fight to promote marginalized voices and create a safe space for developers to work within this industry. Similarly, the space and community surrounding Twine, the program I used to develop both *Stop Me* and *Lights Out, Please*, are inherently political in a way that feels feminist because, at its core, Twine is about accessibility and inclusivity through that accessibility. It is community. For many, it is survival.

Twine creates text-based games similar to a digital choose-your-own-adventure book. Because Twine is free and requires no programming to use, it has been used widely by marginalized creators to tell the stories that are not being shared in mainstream video games, particularly games and stories about being transgender and games and stories about real, lived experiences of mental illness.

Using Twine and creating body horror games about self-dismemberment has been a political move to challenge both what we consider a "game" and the voices and stories we accept as dominant in conversations around mental illness. Games made in Twine often get challenged for not being real games, but also not being real literature, and thus they exist in this liminal space of not enough for any proper categorization and therefore not enough to be considered valid.

This liminal space gives us the freedom of form to share how we want to share and what we want to share and to push back at everything around us that says we are not valid or not enough. Twines are pushing back, giving voice to marginalized creators, giving life to stories that are unlikely to be championed by large, AAA publishers. There are Twines about racism, sexism, transmisogyny, the power of BDSM to heal. There isn't one way to create in Twine, just like there isn't one way to play a game. Video games, games of all sorts, occupy different spaces of play. And no matter what engine you use, what story you tell it, it is enough. And together, we can push back.

By making these games and using dismemberment as a metaphor for what an eating disorder can feel like, I have been able to open an honest and clear dialogue with myself—and with others. It's this dialogue, which necessitates other people, that has allowed for healing and building a community of support with others.

This is radical vulnerability, a critical intimacy with both myself and with others that has informed my practice of being a game developer. Twine, too, is a sort of vulnerability. It lets us, as game developers, see our tensions with games as a medium, with what we consider games and why. And embracing this vulnerability allows for us all to grow, to become better, stronger, more than we were and ever thought we could be.

And community is an integral part of this. Twine wouldn't be what it is without the community backing it, creating within it, using it to challenge, to resist, to subvert, and to claim space. "It's nice to be held by other women who get it," that woman said in my trauma recovery group, but the same thing applies to collaborating and having fun with other marginalized people in games. We don't have to all agree. In fact, it's better when we don't, when we let our disagreements challenge and grow each other. But it is empowering just to be there, in the same space as others, working together and making something cool. Healing can only happen through vulnerability, and this is true of both personal trauma and collective pain.

I make digital games about dismembering my own body because that's the closest way I can explain what it feels like to be filled with such self-loathing and such hot, burning energy that fuels self-harm. And I know what that kind of radical vulnerability means. I know what it's like to inherently dismantle the very foundation of oneself and to rebuild through vulnerability and through connections with others.

I know, because I had no other choice. Embrace vulnerability and speak and heal, or conform to a safety of propriety and discretion and be silenced and never heal. Survival comes in different forms to different people. For me, survival means embracing vulnerability and creating the space for shared experiences in order to build bridges within my community. Radical vulnerability necessarily fights isolation, and if there's one thing I've learned in the five years I've been a game developer, it's this:

We cannot survive alone. And we are alone if we are silenced.

CHAPTER 4

Black Unicorn

Jonathan Jennings

I DIDN'T ORIGINALLY WANT TO be a programmer; I just wanted to make games. There's a lot about my time and experience in this industry that makes me feel like a bit of an unusual suspect in a small industry. There's a very small pool of black developers (steadily growing, thankfully!), and of that small pool of developers I am employed in the smallest discipline. I've met five black game programmers in my 5+ years in the industry, and two of them were at this year's (2017) E3. With that said, though, every day, every project, every year I appreciate the art form and value of programming a little more. When I thought about "making games," of course I envisioned designing an epic hero, creating a tune gamers hum to themselves out of habit, and designing something that people just don't want to put down. In programming I have learned I can help in doing all the above but also be the man behind putting all these pieces together into a complete experience.

My road to a career in game development started like that of most of us in this industry. I was an excited little kid with a controller glued to his hand. My parents, aunts, and uncles would shoo me outside so that I would go play and stop rotting my brain on all these video games and I would … because I knew if I went outside for an hour or two, then when I came back in not too much later, they'd let me and the game I was playing have peace. Growing up, games were just a fun and adventurous outlet; I loved running at ridiculous speeds, saving the wrong people from the right castles, and sneaking around as a spy in a cardboard box. I've always had an overactive imagination, so investing in the deep narratives of two random characters walking across the screen taking out bands of thugs, robots, ninjas, and warriors was extremely easy for me to get into.

As I got older, my fascination/obsession/infatuation with games only increased—and so did my thirst for knowledge on how these titles I enjoyed so much came to be. At one point I was subscribed to five gaming magazines, talking to friends about games all day at school, posting on gaming forums at night, and watching whatever reviews and gaming-related shows I could on G4. I was consumed with all things gaming. Games wouldn't get much space in the magazines, but the few times they had interviews with developers about their positions and how they got into the game industry I would read and re-read the interviews. I had a hard time understanding the connection between the people who made games were, where they made games (in terms of location), and how they got there. I wanted to make games, but I had no clue where to start; it was my junior year in high school when the first commercials for game development degrees started showing up, and when I realized I could go to college and learn how to develop games, I was pretty much sold on what I wanted to study as a young adult.

One thing I have to express is how thankful I am for my mom; my family has gotten better in our technical knowledge through the years, but when I was in high school, I was the family computer expert and I just knew a lot about Microsoft Word. So when I first told her I wanted to make games and she supported me even though it was a world she didn't understand, a world where no one in my family or any of their extended friends could help, and I was driven solely by my passion, it just reminds me how blessed I am to have her in my life. Have no doubts about it, she didn't know if there was anything to this dream either, but she knew I was passionate about it, and that was enough for her to encourage me to do it. I love you momma.

So, I apply to enroll in a Game & Simulation programming curriculum towards the beginning of my senior year, and I know absolutely NOTHING about programming. I just want to make games, and if this code stuff helps me to do it, then great. The school gives me one free course to get my feet wet, which I do every Saturday on the tail end of my senior year of high school, and honestly, those first classes bored me out of my mind. I didn't remember much past writing a "Hello World" program, but again to me this was a stepping stone. If this is what I needed to know to make games, then I was going to learn it.

College overall was great, but freshman year was a lot of unnecessary reiteration of things to me. Remember, I am a game fanatic, so classes that went over different gaming genres were a waste of money. The books would list three games from a genre when I could tell you fifteen that I loved off the top of my head. I did learn a lot more about the different positions available in the industry. My sophomore year was the year I started to get to play with A.I. programming. I learned a lot in my physics and other math classes, and it was the first year I really sank my teeth into programming. I also had a class or two about 3D modeling, just to understand a little about the discipline. My junior year was the year things started to come together, one of the books we were given earlier in the curriculum was called the *Game Maker's Apprentice*,* and it taught you how to make simple games in a 2D engine using code or a drag-and-drop scripting language.

That book helped me create some of my first portfolio projects; a few weekends I would shut myself in and create the games the book recommended, and then, once I had a better grasp of the engine, I'd work on my own small projects later. We also started to play with 3D engines (such as Unreal) my junior year and get into some of the more low-level programming classes. My senior year was my big year, when I had to put my senior project together. I started working on creating an online portfolio to showcase my stuff. I sent my resume out to literally hundreds of studios in California as well as a few in other states just to see if I'd get a response. By the time I graduated, I just knew I was ready to be the next Shigeru Miyamoto and grace the game industry with my brilliance. It sounds so naïve, but my entire career and all my success to that point had been driven by my passion, so I didn't know any better.

Anybody who's graduated with any degree can tell you that the gap between getting your first "real" job and graduating is a rough period, a period that lasted six months for me. I spent a lot of time sending out more resumes (I sent over 300 total before I got my first job) and developing some more small portfolio projects, and every so often I would actually be called in for an interview. I lived about an hour outside of LA, so it typically took over an hour to get to any of the few game studios I was invited to interview at. One thing I learned very quickly when I showed up was that I was not who they expected to see walk through the door.

---

* Habgood, J., Overmars, M. 2006. *The Game Maker's Apprentice: Game Development for Beginners.* Apress, New York. https://www.apress.com/us/book/9781590596159

Black game developers are already a very small minority in game development, and most black developers are artists, producers, or testers. So here I come, this black junior programmer, and the look they gave me can only be described as the kind of look you'd give seeing a unicorn. A few times I felt like there was some hostility or suspiciousness towards me, like I was a con artist who just wanted to take advantage of the studio. A few of my other interviews went the other way almost as if I was some remarkable exotic creature they weren't sure they'd see again so they'd pick my brain but not be as interested in hiring me. I had ten in-person or phone interviews before I got my first job.

The interview that led to my first job was memorable in that I was blown away at how close it was to Venice Beach. I could literally take a two-minute walk from the office front door and be in the ocean. They had dogs running around the office, and two programmers and a producer took me into an office with a big solid wooden table. I was beyond nervous, but I'd looked up the games they had worked on and mentioned how cool they looked; it was very apparent I knew little to nothing about real game development, and my producer let me know that he knew I was the man for the job when I told him I'd be moving in with my grandparents who lived closer if I was offered the job. I believe it was two days later I got my first formal job offer from a game studio, and of course I accepted.

It's been about five and a half years since that time, and I've been a part of the release of about eleven games. The work I've produced has been downloaded over two million times, and now I'm working primarily in the VR (Virtual Reality) space. I've grown a lot, and while my passion is the engine that got me to this point, my curiosity is what has allowed me to stay in game and software development. To most people programming looks boring, and whenever I start dropping technical terms like "variables," "functions," or "instances," I can actually see the glaze coming over the eyes of whoever I am talking to if they aren't a programmer. I absolutely get it, by the way; like I've said, this was never a predefined path for me, and it's not something I was good at as a young teenager. All my programming knowledge and growth has developed over these past nine years of studying and working.

What I've come to love about programming is that it provides me with constant challenges; I'm constantly learning and have to figure out new ways to build features. I get bored easily, so a job where almost every day I'm trying something new or continuing a new part of a large system has been critical for keeping me mentally engaged. The fact that I work on games only amplifies that variety. For example, if for the past three days I've been working on some audio system and putting in soundtracks, I might be working on new gameplay after that, then I might be implementing new art, and then I might be integrating Facebook into the game after all of that.

A game has so many pieces, and being allowed to touch and get all the individual pieces working together in a single environment keeps me entertained. You literally can't "make the game" more than programming, and it's the nature of the job that you are usually plugged into the communication between everyone else. New art needs to be created? The artist is going to ask what the poly count of the model should be. New music is being produced? The producer is going to ask how the audio needs to be cut. A new feature needs to be added? The game designer is probably going to request a meeting with whatever engineer is assigned to it to go over how the mechanic should work and what he needs to polish it once it's in. There's a lot of responsibility that comes with being a programmer, but I also enjoy having such an important part in bringing the game to life.

For me working in the game industry has meant living a childhood dream—and I couldn't be happier. About three years ago at E3 2015, I got to meet one of my gaming idols and one of those men whose interviews I read as a thirteen-year-old in my gaming magazines; that man was Tim Schafer (*Secret of Monkey Island, Grim Fandango,* and *Psychonauts*). It embarrasses me now because we took a picture together, he shook my hand, and when he tried to talk to me I completely froze and barely got my name out. As embarrassing as that was, I can't explain how exciting, fulfilling, awe-inducing, and surreal that moment was to me. If I had any doubts about whether I truly was living my childhood dream, that moment demolished them for me. In the day-to-day I learned pretty early on that nothing about game development is standard; my offices have for the most part been zany spaces with large TVs, game consoles, computers, and dogs all over the place.

I get to sit in on "serious" meetings where we debate the merits of a double jump versus a single jump, where we talk about in-game economies and unlockables, and I can bring up games like *Sonic the Hedgehog* and *Super Smash Bros.* and not just have it be relevant but use those as practical examples of the games we may be looking to produce in the future. Naturally all jobs have their downsides, too; it's pretty difficult to release a game on schedule without putting in some late nights over the course of the project. I've worked weeks where we went seven days straight. I've spent the night at the office; in fact my first three weeks in the industry we averaged more than thirteen-hour work days.

With that said, though, I can recall a number of great memories I had even during those long, intense shifts. That's where I can't understate how awesome it is to work with other game developers. I've made life-long friends from other countries and completely different walks of life who I will always cherish. They started off just as coworkers, but a good number of the men I've worked with have become my brothers and game development family. They make every moment of game development just that much better.

I've really enjoyed writing this; it really took me back to a lot of interesting points in my life, being a game-crazed teenager and an endlessly excited college student. How scary, nerve-wracking, and interesting those first job interviews were. Even now, as I look around my apartment, which is of course littered with game consoles, posters, and game-related art, how my passion and excitement for games has persisted after all these years. I'm

ecstatic about what gaming turns into: as VR grows and develops, the games we play now might not even resemble what we'll be playing ten years from now. I'm most excited to write this in the hopes that some thirteen-year-old reading this will have their own mental light bulb go off and irrational passion for game development stoked. Here's to the next generation of game makers.

CHAPTER 5

Lauren Ashlee Comp

O N THE FIRST DAY of work at my new job—a fresh-faced graduate full of nerves and excitement—I outed myself to the entire studio over lunch. What I didn't know then was the importance of that moment, how it would shape the rest of my time at the company and the trajectory of my entire career. I have been incredibly fortunate in finding not only a workplace that allowed me to thrive, grow, and face new challenges but also a robust community of diverse developers. Or, as I like to call them, friends.

Every person you meet has the potential to change your life. That's what all the epic tales spun to us in narrative-based games say, and while the words may feel eye-roll-worthy, I have found the truth in them. The first people who shape you are your family members, and I believe without my family, cherished and special and close to my heart, I would not be a developer who fights despite being marginalized. My father is a hardworking, blue-collar man who sees the best in everybody, even when they don't deserve it. My deaf mother is a teacher who refuses to accept the limits set by others with the energy of two thousand sugar-rushed children. My older sister—though not in name or blood, but a member of my family nonetheless—aspires to be the most brilliant young black doctor of her time and hasn't stopped chasing that dream, even after becoming a single mother of three. My younger brother is autistic and finds the joy in routines and repetition of colors, movement, noises, and feedback and now harnesses that joy to canvas once a month. This isn't some sort of bingo card of diversity—those don't *exist*. My privilege is and was still very much so real; we were a middle-class family in the 1990s when the middle class still existed, I went to a good school, I had dinner on the table every night, and I was in a family full of love. My family welcomed everyone to our door, any walk of life, and meeting so many individuals with different stories, different lives, changed the way I thought of storytelling from a young age.

The first console I owned was a hand-me-down from my dad's friend— a Sega Genesis with *NHL* and *Sonic* and *Rocket Knight Adventures* that I spent hours playing alone. Tiny pixelated hockey men and two blue rodents didn't give me much to think about in the way of characters, but I did find a sense of challenge and enjoyment I hadn't ever felt before. But it wasn't any of these Genesis titles, or Gameboy, or Nintendo 64, that truly sparked my desire to make games, but *The Sims*.

The Sims was the first game where I could see my sister and me at the same time in one game, a black girl and a white girl who would look and act like us (to the extent they could in the year 2000). It was the first game where I could see glimmers of the identity I would grow into, with two women on the screen kissing. I could create any of a multitude of people and reflect the world my family had been teaching me about, a world of diverse, wonderful people, and I was excited to learn even more. As the years passed, I thought more games would reflect this kind of world, more games would exist where I could see representations of everyone I loved and cared about on screen. It's unfortunate that even now, it's still difficult to find my friends in these stories.

Moving from southeast Michigan to the heart of Tempe, Arizona, expanded my perspective again, introducing me to people who shared my drive to create. My school hosted courses for young and old, people from different countries, different religions, different cultures and ideas bursting with creativity. Then there were the Game Production students, some who slept in every class, some who took notes fervently, some with networks like those of celebrities, and some who had never left their home towns before that very moment. Veterans, wheelchair users who also happened to be athletes covered on ESPN , young Jewish men, Native Americans, a handful of other queer folx like myself, and, luckily enough for me, a mentor who saw that burning desire in my eyes to do something more. The experiences I enjoyed in university were wonderful, but one thing remained core to my being: The world was better with all of us together. And I wanted the same from games.

I made it through three years of schooling, watching some friends leave to return home to brilliant places before graduation, while others stood side by side with me in our graduation robes. We all had dreams, some of us had internships and projects, others wanted to take time to further perfect their skills. I had a family back home who were proud of me, though I was unsure of what I would do next. Fires don't just go out, when the first log is done burning, not when there's a whole pile of pallets ready to light. I applied endlessly, digging deep, tugging on some of the network bonds I had formed, until finally...

On my first day of in what I was proud to call my new career, the one small step into the industry I had been chasing after, I outed myself to the entire studio over lunch. This is where some stories would come to a screeching halt. I am one of the lucky ones, and I dream that this sort of luck will become more common as time passes.

It wasn't until after I had said, out loud, that my at-the-time girlfriend had packed my lunch for me that I realized what I had done. Unlike southeast Michigan, the Midwest at large, or the heart of Arizona, this was San Francisco, California. While the company headquarters may be rooted in Japan, the members of the SF Branch Studio didn't bat an eye. This was apparently a bigger deal than I had even known at the time, as on the next day my *senpai* [meaning upperclassman, or more loosely "someone older than you"] messaged me in secret to tell me she too had a partner and was so happy to have someone else in the office to talk with. That one day, that one lunch, was the first domino in the masterpiece that I am trying to shape my career into.

As an associate producer, it was my job to help in the creation of what our studio did best, romance visual novels. I was pulled onto a newly formed team to help with the next title from the studio: *Queen's Gambit*. After the first three days of orientation, learning more about what the job entailed (plotting, editing, writing, contractor management, art requests, testing, and more) my then-producer pulled me into a room. He thought just maybe, if I was also on board, we could try pitching the *first ever lesbian romance option* in our games. I remember leaning forward in the quiet stillness of the room, looking him in the eyes, and telling him, "You picked the right girl for this job."

Gambit was only meant to be in development for about six months before release, but it was ambitious in the wrong way—trying to build a new engine from scratch. The initial release of *Queen's Gambit* took a year from when I was hired, which is far too long for mobile development given our size. It only launched with two characters, which did NOT include the character I had devoted my life to in that year. **Emily Verma** was the name of the first ever female love interest from our company, and she was my reason for living. It wasn't healthy, the hours I was working, but I "Did It For Her," as the classic *Simpsons* meme says. I even made that my desktop background. I wasn't in a good place physically, emotionally, or mentally, but I was in the midst of following my dream right out the gate from graduation. I couldn't stop, not now. Emily Verma was not just our first ever lady love interest; she was a woman of color as well. Her Indian surname and gorgeous complexion weren't overlooked by our fans, some of whom later went on to tell me it was the first time they had *ever* seen themselves in a game. That's skipping to the victory, though.

The process of getting Emily Verma released to the world was not an easy one. Following the initial release, the game was not well received. It was buggy, the chapters were too long, and it was hard to follow. It was deemed a failure, but it only made me more determined to make Emily's story better, to make it something worth remembering, to make it a story I wish I had growing up—that young women who love women could read and feel like they aren't alone, even when the odds are against them. I had been working mostly on *Queen's Gambit* at this point, though I had been put onto a new and upcoming team with a new project on the side. My heart was in *Gambit*, though the new project was exciting too.

The next month upper management said they wanted to cut their losses and end *Gambit* before Emily could be released. This came the morning I had gotten it all working on device and excitedly shown everyone who would so much as breathe in my direction the moment they walked in the door. Hindsight is supposed to be 20/20. That's what everyone says, at least. Sometimes I question if what I did following that announcement was the right choice. And then I look at the messages, the love, the tears, the emotion fans have expressed over Emily Verma, and I know in my heart I did what I had to.

I'm not necessarily proud of this, but I all but begged. I made deck after deck after deck, each document explaining the costs, what we had already sunk into the content that they would not release. It was so out of my wheelhouse, but I was driven by a mad sort of desperation. I needed the world to see Emily Verma, and the world needed her, too. After so much of my own blood, sweat, tears, exhaustion, mental health, my absolute all went into the content, I couldn't give it up.

I'll never forget the people who backed me up, the people more senior to me who fought my case as well. Without them, Emily Verma would never have seen the light of day. And with tears in my eyes, I was the one allowed to "press the button" and release Emily's content into *Queen's Gambit*—and into the world. It was a victory like no other in my life. The fans loved her, coveted her, played over and over until they got the best endings. Emily's popularity was surprising to everyone but me, because I had just let my heart out into the wild for people to see.

Two months later the entire production team was laid off, with me as the sole exception because I was on the new team. This wasn't a shock to the majority of us; the writing had been on the wall since the initial launch. So while I finished getting Emily released, more and more of my time was spent with this new team, on this new exciting project that, beyond all shadow of a doubt, was also given the thumbs up to include a lesbian love interest. More than that, we were given the freedom to include other diverse characters, more queer background characters, and a nonbinary character who we had big plans for—all of whom, thanks to the overwhelming response from fans, would eventually get their own story.

Astoria: Fate's Kiss, or *Labyrinths of Astoria* as it was known at the time of launch, was a new breath of fresh air compared to *Gambit*. The team was a mix of people who had worked on "US Original" titles, more Americanized stories and art, and the localized titles from our Japan HQ. It was to launch as a new line of titles that bridged the two sets of fan bases with a line name to represent that quite literally, "AmeMix." **Medusa** was a fresh start because, while Emily Verma would forever remain in my heart, Medusa was seen as a strong character who held serious potential for revenue. She lived up to that title by becoming the second best-selling character in the app, preceded only by the character who would be the face of AmeMix until 2017. The whole team was so excited, so free to make our worlds inclusive of the experiences we lived, of the people we knew. We had characters of every race, magical setting be damned. Zeus, Poseidon, and Hades were men of color.

Aphrodite and Persephone were women of color. Aphrodite's left hand proudly wore a hijab after a fan asked if she would ever see herself in our games, as there were no hijabi characters in our games, and very few positive hijabi characters in the games industry at large. I saw their question, so genuine and full of hope and love, and asked my now-producer,

"Why not? Why not include them?," and we did. More and more progress was made, with characters like **Alex Cyprin**, our first and *the only* nonbinary romanceable character in mainstream romance visual novels and one of the only canonically nonbinary characters in the entire gaming world. Our numbers kept growing, and as we prepared the launch of our next title, *Gangsters in Love*, it was no longer a question of *if* there would be a lady love interest, but *who* she would be.

In two years, I had gone from hopeful pipedream to sure-thing inclusion for women who love for women to see ourselves in the games. **Aurora James** was launched to huge fan-hype, and as our first Mexican-American love interest, we were once again able to let my friends see themselves in a way they never had before in games. Following *Gangsters* came *Castaway! Love's Adventure* with **Dr. Serena Zhang**, *Kisses & Curses* featuring **Anastasia Petrova** and **Melanie Harris**, *Love & Legends* with **Altea Bellerose**, and a revival of an old title that my senpai had worked on, *Speakeasy Tonight*, was given an upgrade and included **Sofia Martinez**. *To Love & Protect*, another classic, was completely overhauled to include three times more character of color, as well as a new lesbian love interest **Madison Lane**.

All of this built up and led to *Havenfall Is for Lovers*, a game that I am leading directly as junior producer of my own team. The first character to be announced, and the first character to be released, **Mackenzie Hunt**, is a biracial lesbian town sheriff and werewolf. For the first time, fans won't have to wait to see themselves until the heterosexual characters have been released. They can enter the game immediately and fall in love with another woman, and a Queer Woman of Color (QWOC) at that.

All because on my first day of work, I outed myself to the entire studio at lunch.

After date of writing, six more queer routes have been added to Lovestruck.

Thank you, Tanya, for this opportunity and the hard work you do every day to make games better.

CHAPTER 6

The Creative Compulsion

A Reflection

KN Granger

L ET ME START WITH my privilege labels: cisgender, white, woman, highly educated, straight-passing, raised rich. I'll follow up with my other identities: queer, cis-by-default, semidisabled, mentally ill, currently time and cash poor, fat.

I'm in the gaming industry mostly as an analog tabletop game designer, but sometimes I'm involved in journalistic areas or other artistic endeavors. I got started in this industry both because of these identities and despite them. One of my friends recently commented on the fortitude of my drive. I'm somehow able to conceive of novel projects and execute them, nearly in the same breath. She—and other folks—find it both astonishing and impressive. I find it as natural as a fish crawling up a tree—it's difficult, it's not what I'm supposed to do, and yet for some reason I'm unable *not* to do it. It's both a great strength and a killer weakness. I consider it a compulsion to create.

As a result of this compulsion—or passion, if we're being generous—I have written and made and crafted and devised a whole lot of things—analog games, essays, books, fanfiction, self-help worksheets, syllabi and educational materials, MP3s, videos, websites, paintings, written music… oh, so much stuff. I'm in the process of trying to compile all of my more tangible things into a little bundle. That effort is my website, roseclue.com, where I'd love to bring all these random little things together into a comprehensive whole. It's a work in progress.

But the tragic side effect of my drive—it makes me deeply unhappy. Walter Wellesley Smith said, "Writing is easy. You just open a vein and bleed." He was too right. All of my creating comes from pain of some kind—usually the pain that comes from seeing the absence of *something*. This *something* always strikes me as important, valuable, and needing to exist. And I will often go to great lengths to manifest the creation of *something*—sacrificing sleep, nourishment, hydration, socialization, and the creation of other *somethings*. And of course, these losses have consequences, and of course as soon as I've completed a project, or when I've given up on it, I swear that I'll take better care of myself next time. And then the next *something* comes along, and I'm off to the races again, frenetically chasing whatever *something* I'm after.

In some ways, the pattern I exhibit of seeing an *absence* of *something* and then seeking to fill the space…it might be an example of what Aristotle calls "mimetic inspiration," or the inspiration that comes when you see something done, and you think, "I could do that…with my own style!" Sometimes that instinct is there, in my mind. I will play a wonderful game at a convention, and I'm dazzled, and I am telling everyone about it and thinking about it for the next six months until I take a stab at using some new tools I identified, achieving some semblance of the beauty that the other game captured in terms of mechanics or flavor. "This is a game of *Fiasco* where the flavor is *Welcome to Night Vale!*"

Other times, my compulsion is simply a shocked "Why is there a gap here? Someone could suffer!" In game design, usually this has to do with things like name tags, introductions using pronouns, my favored technique of using the X card, and more. It can sometimes be a matter of "I see that there's a game that combines this technique, and this other technique, but no games that involve both techniques…Let's do it!"

And then I do it. I "do it" a higher percentage of the time than most people, it seems. That's what the compulsion dooms me to—a better batting average, I guess.

The compulsion has taught me a lot about sacrifice. The effort I put into creation has taught me how to plunge forward into the darkness without knowing if the work will ever be good, how to be vulnerable and see joy everywhere I look in the world, how to lose and yet still persevere, how to experience peace in the midst of chaos. How to put one thing above all

else, treasure it, make it grow, let it expand its leaves towards the sun...
and then let it go. The process of artistry is a process that is painful and
beautiful, analogous to childbirth and rearing. And as with children, the
"letting go" is one of the most important parts—permitting the creation
to breathe, to take on a life of its own, to sink or swim on its own merits.
That's what makes it *real*.

But back to this compulsion of which I speak. This compulsion is my
process of artistry. I think part of the reason it poses such a problem for
me is that at the very instant I get an idea, I have a vision of that idea
being actualized. I don't just see "anthology of essays by creative change
pioneers." I see myself researching databases of artists and drafting my
initial introduction email and sending this introduction email to about
two hundred people in an afternoon. And since I so easily see the steps to
complete the project, I do it. And I have done it.

It's like being a little kid. You know that trope in movies where the
adults turn their back for two seconds, and then they turn back around
and see their kid hanging from a tree? That's the perfect image of my artist-
brain. I turn my prudent adult brain around for two whole seconds, and
then I look back and my artist-brain has scrambled up the Eiffel Tower!
Or—more likely—is trying to recreate *The Birth of Venus* starring a fat
lady as Venus.

Darn, that's a cool idea, isn't it?

Notice the *darn* here. It's very revealing. My creativity is a heavy bur-
den, and every new idea seems to have weight equal to every other past
idea that I've had. I can't prioritize my ideas, and I can't file them away and
organize them. So my immediate reaction to new ideas is that I have pain.
Perhaps it's a little cocktail of two kinds of pain: the pain of anticipating
the pain of toil, plus the pain of wanting something desperately.

Some of my greatest accomplishments are a result of this creative compulsion, like my aforementioned anthology about social justice and art. Or
my game, *Ghost Ship Enyo*, which I wrote at an alarming and exhausting
speed. But every time I launch myself into a new project when I'm supposed to be doing something else, and there's a time clock pressing against
that thing I'm *supposed* to do and I just can't bear to break myself away
from the *something* that has captured the whole of my creative attention...
well, I confess it's made me late for things. It's also made me flake on
things entirely, because I'm a silly person who can't prioritize friends over
somethings sometimes. It's not procrastinating—at least not the way most

people talk about procrastination. I consider it an overoptimistic attitude towards time. I sometimes sit staring at the clock, glancing at it every few seconds, seized by the compulsion to write a game, ignoring the fact that I have a Skype meeting in half a minute, and the fact that I desperately need to use the bathroom and have some dinner.

The compulsion to create has a powerful effect on my psyche and the way I relate to the environments around me. I can't turn on the water in the kitchen to fill a pot, walk into the other room, and do something else for a second while the pot fills up. Instead, I'll walk into the other room, get interested in something, and hazily register that the pot is overflowing in the sink, but I'll tell myself, "Just a minute" endlessly until the house is flooded. As a result, I sometimes have anxiety and panic related to certain situations—time to waste means that I'll end up with a flooded house if I'm not extremely diligent.

This compulsion to create—and its effects—permeate beyond the bounds of my miserable little artist's existence. The compulsion has simultaneously meant the following, to me: that I'm always the one at fault, and that I can make things better. It's taken me time to learn that this isn't true, though it's a hard lesson to take.

Here's one vivid example: I was in college, and my "philosophy of film" professor told me that my essay just "didn't make any sense." I'd really been proud of my essay—I'd thought it was very inspired, well organized, and really tied together all the ideas that we talked about in class. And moreover, I had diagrammed out all the sentences to make it as straightforward and logical as possible because of similar feedback on a previous essay.

And I left his office hours that day wondering what the *heck* I had done wrong. Because obviously it was my fault, there wasn't any reason that the philosophy department at my school was so barren of female philosophy majors. There wasn't any reason that all the "successful" students in the class were men. There wasn't any reason that all the subjects we studied in the class were male-directed movies.

I mean, it could be that I was just rubbish at philosophy because of the compulsion leading me astray. At the time, that's clearly what the answer was. The compulsion led me off the beaten track and into mires of mist and moor, where soon I became irretrievably lost.

But the presence of the compulsion blinded me to the now-obvious retrospective: misogyny probably played a larger role in my final grade in that class than any other factor.

It's so easy to let these kinds of experiences become *de rigueur* in this industry, too. I am shamed for not liking "crunchy" games by guys who confuse their personal preferences with objective facts. I have spent hours listening to men wax philosophical about their favorite system, ignoring the fact that I'm giving them the "mannequin challenge." Apparently this is what the cool kids these days are calling "giving a blank stare and not responding."

And it's hard not to cave to the pressure in a male-dominated field. All the key elements of business involve getting past the gatekeepers and massaging the stakeholders—nearly all of whom are men. (Though increasingly not so, of course.) Like the philosophy major at my undergraduate institution, the gaming industry is traditionally kept locked-down and inaccessible to women and nonbinary folx. A lot of the time, in order to get ahead, we have to sacrifice ourselves in order to make the bucks. I see people do it, and do it successfully—using Kickstarter, forming alliances with other industry titans, and other means of moving product.

Unfortunately, the compulsion that I have precludes me from engaging in this element of the business. I'm a creator who doesn't have the capacity or interest to be a seller, a pusher, and, therefore, a winner. I'm a creator who prefers to just mold something together, shove it out into the world without much applause, and then continue to mold things. I like to be the butcher grinding the meat. I don't like to be the sales clerk or cashier.

My products are good, and sometimes they're really great. But sadly, this industry and its infinite smallness isn't one where folks can sink or swim despite their abilities—or disabilities. Like in publishing, unless you've got a great publisher who takes care of everything for you other than the writing (a.k.a. unless you're J.K. Rowling or something), you have to do everything pertaining to marketing and promotion. And that's why we sometimes get mediocre games being widely celebrated, while brilliant jewels of the art get lost in the coal scuttle. There isn't a lot of opportunity for great art to get the visibility it desperately deserves, especially when there are so many artisans just like me.

But what can I do? The compulsion takes me where the compulsion takes me. Trust me, I've attempted to harness it, but I have learned that, for the most part, it takes me good places. Sometimes those places might not feel good—like when I create something that is scorned as "derivative" of something I had no idea existed—but generally I like the results.

I suppose an element of this is: I trust the compulsion. Perhaps I give it too much free rein at times. And perhaps this is the reason I'm not rich off my dozens upon dozens of creations. I suppose that I trust the compulsion to take me somewhere newer and more exciting than the last place it took me. I'm on the journey of my life, an endless pursuit of beauty. If I didn't trust the compulsion, if I doubted the compulsion more, perhaps I would be more prudent and be able to focus on really polishing and selling the products I've created. But the compulsion is just too enticing, and besides—the compulsion and I have been together for a very long time. We have a very healthy dysfunctional relationship, like a garden so overrun with dandelions and milk-thistles it can't help but be beautiful.

I suppose this is the sort of thing that poets write about when they talk about their "muse." I think the compulsion likes to be personified. It's a very natural instinct to personify it, for the compulsion feels so much like an external force, not at all like a series of misfiring neurons and over-active brain chemicals. It feels like something that must be obeyed, upon pain of death. And me? I am obedient to the compulsion, and it rewards me with new things I've never seen before. And hopefully things the world has never seen before.

To be honest, the world will probably never see these things because the compulsion has me trapped among its thorns and brambles.

(But I love it here.)

CHAPTER 7

Laundromat vs. Pizza Place

Shareef Jackson

M Y MOM WAS NOT happy when our washer stopped working, but I was excited. We'd pack our laundry into the car and head over to the neighboring town that had a nicer laundromat. I helped her with the bags and kept my eyes on the prize: the Nintendo *PlayChoice-10* arcade cabinet that stood in the middle of the room.

The machine was 25 cents to play, and luckily, my mom always had a roll of quarters to use on the laundry. I was a great beggar, so I was able to get my fair share of quarters to jump on some Goombas for a few minutes. If I wasn't playing, I would watch someone else—usually a person of a different ethnicity. In my mostly African American and Latinx hometown of Paterson, I rarely (if ever) came across white children hanging out in my neighborhood.

Fair Lawn has a higher percentage of white people than Paterson does—approximately 80% vs. 30% as of the 2010 census. This laundromat was one of the few times that I could interact with a white kid who shared my love of *Mario*. This affected me from a curiosity perspective but never prevented me from interacting. I was worried that the kid might see me as a poor, dangerous criminal from the hood, but not to the point of inaction. Nothing would stop me from playing *Mario*.

The *PlayChoice* wasn't the only option. Just a few doors down, an Italian pizza place had two arcade games—*Crime Fighters* and *RoboCop*. I was nervous in this establishment, for two main reasons. My limited experience with kids who were not black or Latino was negative, and the mafia movies of the day were not shy about using racial epithets against African Americans. I never had any actual bad experiences in the pizza place, but I felt like I could—which was constantly on my mind.

The remnants of my optimistic laundromat experience and pessimistic pizza place experience have been factors throughout my adult life. I went to a predominantly white high school. I felt like I needed to be "down" and represent my city, which led me to publicly shy away from some of the geekier video game stuff that I was into. By doing this, I missed a chance to truly connect with friends of different backgrounds. Pessimism reared its ugly head, and it cost me. That sense of regret led me to be more confident about my geeky self, regardless of who was around, from that point forward.

In college, I shifted from pizza place pessimism to laundromat optimism. I was more comfortable with my detailed knowledge and love of video games than I ever was in high school. I made friends that I might not have even spoken to if not for our shared love of obscure gaming details. I attended long marathon gaming sessions and loved every minute of it. This brought me closer to some folks and ostracized me from others. I saw this as a blessing in disguise since I didn't want to be friends with people that did not accept my full self.

My corporate work life had remnants of both pessimism and optimism. I never saw work as a place to make friends, so I did not share any video game interests with my mostly white colleagues. Occasionally someone else from work stumbled upon my video game podcast or YouTube videos, and this often led to awkward conversations. A mix of amazement and condescension left a bad taste in my mouth after each inquisition. However, I did end up making a few friends, and we talked about video games quite a bit.

Fed up with corporate life, I started my own math and physics tutoring business in late 2016. I'm confident enough in my tutoring skill that optimism guided me through the frustration of leaving my nice, comfy corporate paycheck. I use video games often in my tutoring examples, and I've had parents and students remark that they are surprised at my knowledge. I can't help but shake the feeling that their perplexed statements have to do with my being African American.

In the last few years, I've been blessed with opportunities to mingle with some of the most respected people in the gaming industry. I've been able to interview some of these people on the SpawnOn.Me podcast and dive deep into issues of diversity in my GamingLooksGood.com YouTube series. The same optimism that I felt at the laundromat has been present consistently in the majority of my interactions. Many people involved with making games are about love and support, and they are not afraid to show it.

However, I can't say that is true of other gamers who are not as involved with the industry; the pessimistic side definitely creeps in. The content creation that I have contributed to has often spurred comments from other gamers, many of which have been racially tinged. These comments almost universally use the n-word and make some reference to "the ghetto," slavery, 40s, or a variety of other date stereotypes. The gamers who made these comments have been a variety of ages and come from across the gender spectrum, but many have been white presenting (according to their profile pictures at least). Some of it was so bad that I have questioned if sharing content publicly is worth it. But then, I remember that I create content because it makes me feel good to contribute to gaming culture in my own way. There will always be haters.

Throughout my life, I've constantly returned to my days of the laundromat vs. the pizza place when it comes to being a marginalized person in the gaming industry. Some days are better than others, but overall, it is a large part of my life that I wouldn't give up for the world. Whether you enjoy Nintendo *PlayChoice-10* or *RoboCop*, the world is yours. Don't give up on yourself and your dreams because of the interaction of optimism and pessimism.

CHAPTER 8

The Prevailing Need to Push for Protagonists of Color

Kadeem Dunn

CONTENTS

T HE OTHER DAY, I was speaking to my father on the phone. Amidst the usual back and forth about why I was behind on my bills, still looking for a "steady job," and generally not in the seat of a glamourous life, he asked, "Are you done with the 'game stuff'?"

I brushed off the comment (I hadn't brought up anything about games anyways) and continued towards the end of the conversation. At the time it seemed fleeting and unimportant, but evidently his question has stuck me with me.

I found myself asking: why *am* I choosing to be an independent game developer, especially when it often seemed that there were not enough resources in my life to support the work? I've been told in conversations that the experiences and realities of people of color (PoC) are not marketable or "would have no audience" when it comes to video games and digital culture. As I've discovered and rediscovered in my life as a game designer so far, I choose to be a game designer because, for many reasons, **it makes a difference that I do.**

These days especially, it's so easy to forget that life is bigger than the moment. As humans, we have the power to present our thoughts in ways that are remembered for generations. Think about Aristophanes or Lao Tzu, who wrote works that other humans have been reading for over two millennia. Remember that your audience is larger than the here and now.

Getting my foot in the door as an independent game designer has been a tenuous balance between finding time to work on my projects and finding time to work to cover living expenses. People often ask why I don't get a full-time job and develop on the side. The short answer is I that I've tried many times, and personally I can't pull it off without having the quality of my work deteriorate in both fields of work. As an indie designer, smaller team sizes mean greater responsibilities for individuals within the team. It follows that building an indie game in any sizable time window lands the workload somewhere close to a full-time job. It took building my first game, *Class Rules*, to truly recognize the amount of time and effort that goes into designing and building games.

Without the resources to keep the lights on, the computer running, and food in your belly, you won't be getting very far towards releasing your game. Unfortunately, the numbers show that PoC are more likely to encounter situations where they do not have access to the necessary resources. As Quinland Anderson, a business teacher from the UK said regarding his PoC students, "They often don't have some of the most basic of resources at home that many of us take for granted." At the same time, through whatever means it may be, many Black people feel they have the expertise to succeed but do not see this reflected in the makeup of the industries that they seek employment with.* These are the very real barriers that class and race present—what do you do when you simply can't afford to develop digital games, yet know you have the expertise to do so?

THE "BLACK CANADIAN EXPERIENCE"

A little while ago I had the pleasure of reading some of the stats from *Towards Race Equity in Education: The Schooling of Black Students in the Greater Toronto Area*, a York University study by Dr. Carl James about the lives of Black students in the Greater Toronto Area (GTA).† Folks that

---

* Ramanan, C. "The Video Game Industry Has a Diversity Problem—but It Can Be Fixed." *The Guardian*, Guardian News and Media, 2017, www.theguardian.com/technology/2017/mar/15/video-game-industry-diversity-problem-women-non-white-people.
† James, C.E. & Turner, T. (2017). *Towards Race Equity in Education: The Schooling of Black Students in the Greater Toronto Area*. Toronto, Ontario, Canada: York University.

are not from Canada may not know much about the "Black experience" here, but Black Canadians exist in a vacuum of data about both our present and historical existence.

Without data, we have to base our experience off of a series of "close enough" cases (usually from our neighbors below the color line), which contributes to normalizing the denial of the Black Canadian assertion that our experience with racism is in ways as substantial within Canada as it is with our American neighbors across the border. Black Canadians are often faced with the argument that "Black people have it pretty good" in Canada or that racism does not affect the daily life of many Black Canadians.

Towards Race Equity in Education asserts that **Black students who had a Black teacher in high school were 39% less likely to drop out of school**, which resulted in a 29% increased interest in postsecondary education.[*] To reiterate, it makes a student over a third less likely to drop out of school by just seeing someone who looks a little more like them on the other side of the desk.

The report goes on to explain that part of the reason for that correlation between Black teachers and their ability to encourage Black youth to be more interested in school may be because Black teachers are **over three times more likely to recommend a Black student to a gifted program** than their non-Black counterparts.

The fact is, just by existing as an indie game designer, you are helping to change the environment for younger designers. This is especially true of designers of color. The moment we give up on ourselves is the moment we give up on those that may be inspired by us and go on to do things far greater than we can imagine.

For better or worse, I think this has become a central theme and driving force of my work—making sure that what I create is active in working to normalize the thoughts and perceptions of PoC in popular discourse.

As Canadian rapper Shad puts it in his song *Brother*:

So what the new black activists do for freedom,
Is just being them—do what you're passionate to[†]

---

[*] James, C.E. & Turner, T. (2017). *Towards Race Equity in Education: The Schooling of Black Students in the Greater Toronto Area*. Toronto, Ontario, Canada: York University, p. 65.

[†] Shad. 2007. *Brother (Watching)*, Featured artist: B&F Kabango, Album: The Old Prince, genius. com/Shad-brother-watching-lyrics.

THE FACTS

As in the case with many of the forces that shape our everyday perspectives, experiences, and beliefs, there is a pervasive problem with identity and representation within the video game world. According to Ramanan, "Representation is still very much a problem."[*]

Let's cut to the chase. Here are the hard facts: Latinos, women, blacks, and children are underrepresented in games, while whites and Asians are overrepresented.[†]

But we know this. We've heard many times how negative and prejudicial depictions of PoC in the media have an effect on how PoC are perceived and even think of themselves.

It has been scientifically, sociologically, and psychologically proven that how a certain group is portrayed in the media—the stream of images, videos, and dialogue we interact with on a daily basis—will affect the way they are perceived in other "real-life" situations over time.

George Gerber helped to define this as part of his "cultivation theory." In very broad strokes, there is both a cyclical and dialectical influence between what we see and how we act; the result is that groups with less representation end up participating less in the formation of the representation, which again in turn suggests they will be represented less in the media as well. One can observe how the relationship between prejudices in reality and the media interact with and feed off each other. Some communication theorists argue that "the media work as a mirror for existing social forces as much as a causal agent of them."[‡]

This has a tangible effect on our lives. We internalize the many messages we are bombarded with. In many ways, it can be said that we become what we see. Something worth noting is that in the United States, **Latino and Black children have been shown to play games at the highest rates of all children**. This means that, even though children of color are playing games the most, they are far less likely to see themselves represented.

---

[*] Ramanan, C. "The Video Game Industry Has a Diversity Problem—but It Can Be Fixed." *The Guardian*, Guardian News and Media, 2017, www.theguardian.com/technology/2017/mar/15/video-game-industry-diversity-problem-women-non-white-people.

[†] Williams, D. et al. "The Virtual Census: Representations of Gender, Race and Age in Video Games." *New Media & Society*, vol. 11, no. 5, 2009, p. 824.

[‡] Williams, D. et al. "The Virtual Census: Representations of Gender, Race and Age in Video Games." *New Media & Society*, vol. 11, no. 5, 2009, p. 814.

Further, when they are represented, they are far less likely to exist in primary, narrative, or noncriminal ways.*

Despite all of these negative aspects of media and representation, there is some good news: Representation is a double-edged sword. Just as less representation can lead to further social isolation of these groups, the exact opposite can be said of access to greater representation. That is to say: If creators make the effort to portray PoC positively in the media, this will lead to an even greater amount and diversity of PoC being portrayed in the future.

THANK GOD FOR T'CHALLA

To see an example of this in action, look no further than Chadwick Boseman's landmark performance of Black Panther in *Captain America: Civil War*. I think one of my favorite experiences about the movie was expressed in a very short exchange I overheard in the theater after the movie had ended. As a white father and his two white sons were leaving, he remarked to them, "I don't think Black Panther can carry his own movie."

My mind coursed with a flurry of insinuating questions—"Because it's set in Africa?" "Because T'Challa is not in a relationship with Scarlett Johansson?" "Because Black Panther is—BLACK?"

To my amazement and relief, the children replied together with a resounding denial of their father's assertion. "Yes he can!" they said at once. The kids knew, just as I did, that in all respects, Black Panther is a *fucking badass*. Didn't you see how he scratched Cap's shield with his claws or beat the shit out of Nega Bucky *without his suit*? Logically, if you are a fan of Captain America, Iron Man, and Doctor Strange and think they can hold their own movies, what would lead you to believe that Black Panther couldn't—especially after watching his performance in *Civil War*?

What could it be other than the fact that Black Panther is African? I can't read minds, but perhaps there are those who consider Black Panther's "being African" to be too much of an "other" experience to be relatable to most other movie-goers in America.

This is something I've witnessed first-hand in the world of game education, as well as through the work of education activists like Jane Elliott:

---

* Williams, D. et al. "The Virtual Census: Representations of Gender, Race and Age in Video Games." *New Media & Society*, vol. 11, no. 5, 2009, p. 820.

race is a fabricated concept that is made and taught by human beings. Only through consistent reinforcement of race as a tangible and determinative substance do people learn to use it to navigate everyday life or as a platform for prejudice. A huge part of this conditioning is put in place in childhood. The bright side is that what we learn we can unlearn. Just like the kids at the movie theater exemplify, kids having the freedom to aspire to heroes who—Black, white, or Dark Elf—represent what they see in themselves is a true blessing and evidence of lasting change.

Really, what I've been attempting to communicate is that **more diverse representation matters.** Representation has effects. Researchers have shown that "diversity enhances creativity."* This was evident in the conversation I overheard between the movie-going father and his sons. Through the simplest of exchanges, I witnessed perceptions of two different generations—both the will to grow and the resistance to change. For me, the best part about it all is that the more people who watch a movie like *Black Panther,* the more people who will be more likely to create more content like it in the future.

At the end of the day, this is just the beginning of the type of change we need to see in both Hollywood and the digital game and other entertainment industries. *Black Panther* is a great example of how positive representation of PoC can both result in and illuminate tangible changes in people's perceptions and actions. However, while providing great insight into how relationships between representation and film may engender change in perceptions, it doesn't help to illuminate how the game industry might reflect similar issues.

RACE IN THE GAME INDUSTRY

So, what is the low-down on race relations in games, anyways?

Most of this data comes from a journal article titled "The virtual census: representations of gender, race and age in video games" by Williams et al., which appeared in the journal *New Media & Society* in 2009. Nine years have passed since that article, but that does not mean that the relations among gender, race, and age have changed. These stats pertain to the United States and only tangentially represent the experience of Black Canadians. As was touched on earlier, it follows that some of the statements being made don't apply in the same way to the Canadian context.

---

* Phillips, K.W. "How Diversity Makes Us Smarter." *Scientific American*, www.scientificamerican.com/article/how-diversity-makes-us-smarter/.

That being said, we can still draw similar conclusions from the ratios and correlations that are presented. Further, I think the fact that these relations haven't changed substantially since this journal article appeared is indicative that it is still completely necessary to proactively work towards changing these relationships.

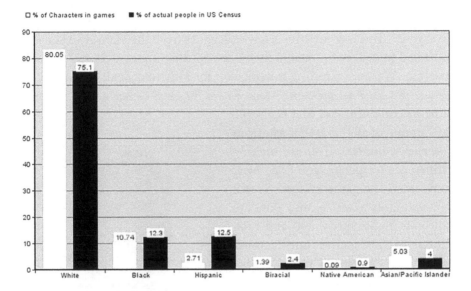

This figure shows that First Nations/American Indians and Hispanics are by far the most underrepresented groups in video games. Contrary to what I stated earlier, Blacks do not seem to be underrepresented by a substantial amount—perhaps slightly less than their actual population, but they're nowhere near as underrepresented as other minorities.

Puzzlingly, **Blacks are actually substantially overrepresented**, particularly when it comes to ESRB-rated "Everyone" titles. Why might this be? The answer is predictable—most sports games are rated "E" for Everyone. And man, black people sure are great at sports.

I held a contest called the "DO YOU WANT TO BE IN A VIDEO GAME?" contest as part of the development of *Class Rules*. The contest challenged entrants to name any black video game protagonist that was:

1. Not from a professional sports game

2. Not a create-a-character

3. Not a fighting game character

The idea was to find out how many black characters in games are in primary, story-driving roles. The results were illuminating.

Without including sports games, it becomes incredibly difficult to find blacks in leading roles. Even more difficult is trying to find blacks in non-sports games with leading roles in games that are rated "Everyone." This is even more surprising considering the previously cited figure that conveys the fact that there is an overrepresentation of Blacks in games rated "Everyone." This is something a few colleagues from the Hand Eye Society and I had to deal with personally while coordinating our Game Curious program. We were running a workshop for kids that dealt with race in games, and *Michael Jackson's Moonwalker* for Sega Genesis was the only game we could think of that fit the bill.

The point of all this is that **what you experience matters**. You are making a difference for people you don't even know exist. The game industry is still very young as a whole, and PoC are still both underrepresented and misrepresented in games and gaming culture. So anytime a question like *"Why am I still doing this?"* crosses your mind, remember the reasons that don't have to do with yourself, your environment, or even those around you. Remember, the world is much bigger than the here and now.

CHAPTER 9

Game Design Is Not a Luxury

Kat Jones

*For women, then, poetry is not a luxury. It is a vital necessity of our existence. It forms the quality of the light within which we predicate our hopes and dreams toward survival and change, first made into language, then into idea, then into more tangible action.**

I REMEMBER READING AUDRE LORDE's piece "Poetry Is Not a Luxury" as an undergraduate. Although I understood what she was saying, I didn't really get it until I became a game designer. Game design, like poetry for Audre Lorde, is my way to communicate with the world. It is my medium of choice for exploring my experiences, observations, hopes, and dreams.

Game design started as a hobby, something to squeeze into my limited free time, a way to deal with writer's block while working on my dissertation. But it has taken up more and more of my time and energy. And as I shift my priorities to make more time for my game design, the question arises: Should I be doing game design full-time?

Making a living as a game designer is a step I have hesitated to take because it requires so much time, energy, and knowledge with limited guarantee of returns. If I was working a job that I found both fulfilling and

---

* All extract in this chapter from Lorde, Audre. Poetry Is Not a Luxury. 1985. https://makinglearning. files.wordpress.com/2014/01/poetry-is-not-a-luxury-audre-lorde.pdf (retrieved August 13, 2017).

profitable, perhaps this question wouldn't come up so often. I'd be content to let game design occupy the nonwork spaces of my life. Yet working as an adjunct professor for little more than nothing, I find myself listening to the siren song of making game design my profession. I wouldn't be sacrificing much in terms of pay, but the potential rewards—the ability to focus a much larger portion of my thoughts, time, and energy on something I find incredibly rewarding—seem vast.

Yet, my hesitation remains. As a designer of analog games, mostly live-action and tabletop role-playing games, there are less profitable options open to me than if I were a video game designer. And the risks I would take on are more than just financial.

The farthest external horizons of our hopes and fears are cobbled by our poems, carved from the rock experiences of our daily lives.

I moved to Western Massachusetts for graduate school in 2003. I didn't realize then that I would soon become part of a vibrant community of indie game designers. Having mentors who were women, including other queer women of color, would give me the courage I needed to enter the field.

The first game I designed "from scratch" was just for fun. I had returned from Fastaval in Denmark inspired by the freeform games I had played. Riding back and forth from my fieldwork in Boston, I listened over and over to Joan Osborne's version of "Man in the Long Black Coat" and decided to write a game about the residents of a small town dealing with the appearance of a mysterious figure sent to offer them judgment or redemption. Players enact various scenes in which they develop their relationships with each other and encounter The Man in the Long Black Coat during his visit.

But as I continued to design games, my games changed. I realized that games were not only a way to tell stories and have fun; they were also a way to explore complex topics, encourage action, and promote change. I still write games that I want to play, but I have expanded my reach to themes and issues that a few years before I would have rejected as game material. Games have become a way to communicate and challenge things I find frustrating: hegemonic beauty standards, parenting advice, gentrification. They are a way for me to explore issues I study and teach using a different lens: feminisms, marginalization, emotional labor. I began keeping a notebook of game ideas in my purse, jotting down things that I felt would make good games: TV shows, movies, real-life encounters, radio interviews, and more.

We can sometimes work long and hard to establish one beachhead of real resistance to the deaths we are expected to live, only to have that beachhead assaulted or threatened by canards we have been socialized to fear or by the withdrawal of those approvals that we have been warned to seek for safety.

Contemplating making a living as a game designer is a frightening thing. Especially if one is a marginalized creator. To stay true to my vision, my reason for designing games in the first place, must I also deny myself the ability to make money with my games?

My options as an analog designer are few. First, I could attempt to be hired by an indie game studio and do work for them while also working on my own games. Second, I could go freelance and attempt to cobble together enough different small jobs for individual projects. Finally, I could enter the realm of Kickstarter or Patreon and attempt to market my own games for profit.

Yet these options all seem to call for some introduction of the market into my design. And I worry how that will impact the games I write. Will I soften my critique to make a game more palatable for a mass market? How will my weird little games survive in the marketplace?

It's hard to know how realistic my fears are. After all, if my games are manifestations of "what we feel within and dare make real (or bring action into accordance with), our fears, our hopes, our most cherished terrors," sharing them beyond a small circle of players feels like a terrifying form of vulnerability. At the same time, many of my fears are based on the experiences of friends who are also marginalized game designers or things I have witnessed myself within the game design community. While I'm not against receiving compensation for my games—I know that I've worked hard to create them and believe that work should be fairly compensated—I'm also wary about how making them a commercial product will change them, and me, in ways I cannot support.

For within structures defined by profit, by linear power, by institutional dehumanization, our feelings were not meant to survive.

Friends who have worked as freelancers complain about the misogyny that is still common in many game companies. Shared stories and experiences help separate companies that treat freelancers with respect from those that perpetuate unequal power relations, further narrowing the pool of companies and individuals I would be willing to work with. Personal experiences witnessing people of color or queer folks being asked to tone down their critique for mass market audiences also makes me skeptical about how I would be asked to change my ideals in these situations.

And while I understand, and support, the importance of creating increased representation for marginalized folks in more mainstream properties like *World of Darkness*, *Dungeons & Dragons*, or others, I am simply not interested in making a living off that form of game design myself. One of the things I love about game design is my ability to focus on the issues and themes that I find important, approach them in ways I find interesting, and offer my own perspective on action and change. Writing for an established game, like D&D, would not allow me the freedom I cherish as a designer.

But what about options like Patreon or Kickstarter? On the surface, these options would allow me both the freedom to focus on my own work and the ability to share this work with a larger audience. While the experience of writing a game is powerful, my games are meant to be played. They truly come to life when they are read and experienced by others.

Yet Patreon and Kickstarter require an amount of public relations, personal branding, and social media engagement that I find daunting. A friend who attempted to go full-time as a game designer explained to me that she quit partly because the money was too unreliable, but also because she found the amount of time she spent on social media—engaging with other game designers, promoting her own games, and searching for potential projects—too overwhelming.

Self-promotion is a difficult skill, one that is not necessarily correlated with being a good game designer. To make a living as a game designer, I would be required to develop myself as a brand, learn the basics of marketing and public relations, and maintain a social media presence on an often hostile Internet. Horror stories of doxing, death threats, and overbearing trolls appear whenever marginalized folx discuss their experiences on the Internet. Tales of unsuccessful Kickstarters or a decrease in audience when games feature queer themes, women, or POC also add to my hesitancy to release my games more fully to the public.

The quality of light by which we scrutinize our lives has direct bearing upon the product which we live, and upon the changes which we hope to bring about through those lives. It is within this light that we form those ideas by which we pursue our magic and make it realized.

So where does that leave me? I know that game design is not a luxury. I know that I want to continue using my games to pursue my magic and make it realized. I recognize that in many ways I am in a privileged position; my job as an adjunct—while limited in terms of salary—gives me the flexibility to pursue game design, attend conferences and conventions, and organize gaming events. My partner's salary is enough that I could attempt to do game design full-time without jeopardizing my family's wellbeing. I'm well connected in the indie game design community and have folks who would mentor me if I asked.

At the same time, as a queer woman of color writing games from that perspective, I still feel incredibly vulnerable when contemplating the attempt to "make a living" as a game designer. While being a game designer is an important part of my identity, at the moment it is only one of many that I hold central to who I am. While it might be easy to explain my hesitance as simply that of any artist trying to make a living with their art, there are real structural factors that impact my decision and lead to my reluctance to become more involved in the game design profession.

Kickstarter and Patreon have opened up new options for a wider range of artists and creators. Yet they are not perfect. There are still ways in which designers with marginalized identities remain marginalized in the game design community, and projects focusing on these marginalized experiences often receive less support—when they are not the subject of open hostility.

Not everyone needs to be a full-time game designer. Not everyone needs to make a living writing games. But we need better ways to support our creators. While game design is not a luxury, it is also not just a hobby. There need to be ways to honor the labor done by game designers, ways to support their work, that are less tied to profits and institutionalized power. Our games give us "the strength and courage to see, to feel, to speak, and to dare." And that is not a luxury, but a necessity.

CHAPTER 10

Hadeel al-Massari

I WAS NEVER FORTUNATE ENOUGH to own the Nintendo Entertainment System growing up, but my grandmother had one, and I spent hours every holiday holed up in the attic with my younger brother and older sister playing *Excite Bike*, *T&C Surf Designs*, and, of course, *Mario*. My grandmother had *Dr. Mario* and the *Mario Bros.* game, but I absolutely favored *Dr. Mario*. There was something about stacking those damn pills that was so satisfying! And if I'm honest, the second level of *Mario Bros.* kind of scared me, but I was only six, so who could blame me for passing on that one for a while?

My love of Nintendo and video games never really waned. I eventually got the original GameBoy one Christmas with a copy of *Tetris* and *Centipede*. I played the entire holiday, and it almost made the entire drive between Portland and Northern Washington, but the batteries died, which was a thing that happened back then and was immensely tragic. I was just the right age for the *Pokémon* boom, and I can't even tell you how many times I beat the Elite Four (Bulbasaur was always my starter, except for my runs through *Pokemon Yellow*), and I seemed to grow up right alongside Nintendo's series of handmade systems. Fast forward through to my senior year of high school; I told everyone who'd listen that I was going to work at Nintendo one day, and this wasn't an uncommon dream. We never knew *what* we wanted to do, but we wanted to do *something* in the House That Mario Built.

Sometimes, dreams really do come true. I found myself selling everything I couldn't fit in the only suitcase I owned and hopping on a cross-country flight to Seattle. Pulling up to Nintendo's Redmond campus was one of the most surreal experiences of my life. In comparison to next-door neighbor Microsoft, Nintendo is tiny. It's tucked away on a quiet, tree-lined side street, the main building separated from an annex by a pristine soccer field. Nothing about the facades makes it scream, "Hey, Mario was made here!" The main building has a much more modern theme than its annex, which could honestly do with a makeover, and the parking garage kind of looks like a jail. The only thing that's going to tip you off to where you are is the single understated sign out front: A sleek white rectangle with rounded edges and the Nintendo logo in dove gray on its face. The inside of the main building is a little more "we make video games," but even the interior's changed drastically since Nintendo stopped offering tours to the public.

Decor aside, sometimes dreams turn out to be nightmares. My time with Nintendo was not a pleasant one. Like many tech and game companies in the area and in fact in the industry as a whole, Nintendo utilizes contract employees. The life of a Nintendo contractor is a rough one. Your contract company will tell you one thing but then do another. Many employees are scheduled for only 39.5 hours a week, so they don't have to be provided with health insurance or benefits. Contractors are not permitted to use Nintendo facilities such as the gym or the pristine soccer field. Contractors aren't even permitted to go into Nintendo's mini-museum, a circular room that has original consoles and cabinets and awards and trophies, which I thought was the most bizarre rule because this museum is literally just a hallway, but if you linger too long, your ass'll get shuffled out in a hurry. It wasn't uncommon to see contractors waiting in the cold parking lot at 5 a.m., having traveled over an hour plus by bus from Renton or Bothell, so they wouldn't be late. Even being two minutes late was seen as a pretty serious offense, and everyone seemed to know someone who got stuck in traffic one too many times only to get an email informing them that their contract had been "completed" as they pulled into the parking lot. Nintendo was kind of a revolving door, and everyone just kind of accepted that, including me. We all told ourselves they just didn't want to be here as much as we did; they weren't as dedicated as we were.

The culture at Nintendo was no better, and I joined just as Gamer Gate was ramping up. My job itself was extremely emotionally taxing, and adding Gamer Gate on top of it made each day feel like a Sisyphean task. I'd push the boulder up the mountain, only to trip on a Gamer Gate–related incident, and that boulder would roll back down the mountain. I'd grit my teeth, push it up again, only to stumble on a coworker referring to a woman in another department as a "slut" or using a racial slur, and down I'd go. No matter how much I loved Nintendo, no matter how much I loved their games, eventually that boulder rolled right over me. I had to leave. It was hard; I felt like a failure, and the relationships I fostered while there slowly faded away. The Mushroom Kingdom didn't seem as magical to me anymore, Hyrule lost its sparkle, and I didn't pick up a video game for almost a year after I left.

When I was ready, it was *Animal Crossing* that welcomed me back. It could have been any other game, any other publisher, but there is something to be said about the worlds Nintendo creates. Using contractors is not unique to Nintendo, and my experience in games as a woman and a person of color is not unique to Nintendo. What I experienced was and still is an industry-wide problem that very few people who are in the position to change it are willing to address. I didn't realize this until I was sitting on my sofa, weeding my very neglected village, when I came to realize how important it was that I keep fighting—for myself, for other women who want to work in games, for people of color. Maybe it seems a little fluffy, but my villagers' happiness at seeing me return after so long lit this little spark in me that led me to teach myself how to code, to connect with other women and people of color in the industry, to support them and lift them up because they need it.

The games side of Nintendo creates a special kind of magic within those unassuming walls. It's the kind of magic that makes you believe that you matter, that you can do great things, no matter what your starting point is. It's the kind of magic that stays with you, even after years and years or even just nine months of wallowing in your own self-pity at imagined failure, that waits for you until you're ready to use it. And it's the kind of magic that welcomes you home. It saves you your spot. It lets you press "A" to continue.

Each day, I'm seeing more and more magic being done on an indie scale, but I'm also seeing more women in programming roles, I'm seeing more people of color visibly managing entire game franchises, and I'm seeing more stories being told from perspectives that need to be represented most. I hear stories similar to mine, which both saddens me but makes me feel less alone, about racism and sexism in the industry and horrible work environments. But we keep going because we all want to be a part of the magic that we all experienced at some point of our lives; we all have memories of being glued to the little TV screen in our grandma's attic every summer. There's a lot of work to be done in the games industry, much of which will be tireless and thankless, and we'll ask ourselves why we're doing it, but it's because we grew up living thousands of adventures through video games, and we know how to beat the final boss by now.

CHAPTER 11

Steven Spohn

O NE OF MY FAVORITE stories from the archives of AbleGamers is from a long-term living center here in the Pittsburgh, Pennsylvania area. We had been working with the local Center for Assistive Technology (CAT) for a long time, fulfilling many wishes and grants, but one day a very special case came into my life. A young man, barely 16 years old, named Zane had received his Make-A-Wish, and what he wished for was the ability to play video games with his brother. CAT pulled us into the conversation as the experts in technology and video gaming.

On a cold winter's day, I rolled through some ridiculously thick snow to meet Zane, his nurses, his orthopedic therapist, his physical therapist, his speech therapist, and his driver. It was quite the entourage. All of them eager, wide-eyed, ready to learn about all that technology had to offer. We sat in a small room surrounded by switches and antiquated technology stored by CAT discussing his dreams of being a race car driver and whooping his brother's butt in *Assassin's Creed*.

Although everyone in the room was excited, you could feel the tension from Zane's group. He sat in his wheelchair, Dynavox (a computerized speaking device controlled by the user's eyes) sat in front of him, giving him the ability to have computerized speech, partially obstructing his view. His natural voice was barely a whisper. The ventilator that had kept him alive all these years also stole his ability to project his voice. Years of fighting a debilitating disease that I know all too well, spinal muscular atrophy, had robbed him of the ability to do anything more than move his eyes, a few fingers, two toes, and his tongue.

It didn't take long before his case became very personal to me. Not only did this kid have the same disease as me, but I could feel his pain. He desperately wanted to play video games like all of the young people around him, even his brother, and he couldn't because of the physical barriers presented by a disability he never asked for. I could see myself in Zane.

The weeks moved forward as we worked together and gathered equipment, supplies, video games, and controllers. AbleGamers wasn't a large organization, at the time. We couldn't afford to foot the $7500 grant cost. And we didn't need to; it was his wish, and Make-a-Wish was footing the bill. However, that meant that we were at the mercy of their queue time. Meanwhile, Zane continued to exchange emails with me, asking questions and learning about this new world of assistive technology. I sent him games that he could play only with his eyes on the device that he already had, which amounted to games like checkers and chess, but he was happy, if not more than anxious. A good feeling would come soon; we both knew it. We just had to get there.

A few days later we got the call that the requisition order I had placed for Zane was approved. Make-a-Wish had come through on their promise to deliver the equipment. It was sent to CAT, and I quickly dove in the day it arrived, eagerly putting parts together and preparing the package for delivery. The morning that it was delivered I can only explain to you that it was nothing short of a miracle. Zane, who was often prone to spouts of fatigue, stubbornness, and grumpy behavior, as most of us were in our teens, was suddenly transformed into the most well-behaved and excited kid I had ever met. He waited patiently as we assembled the equipment and loaded up *Assassin's Creed* and *Forza 4*. His therapists and nurses cried tears of joy.

Zane's entire family lives in a different state, and they never come to visit. They believed that the facility outside of Pittsburgh was his best bet for a good life. And maybe they were right, but it often left him extremely lonely. But what about his brother? Well, his brother also has a form of muscular dystrophy, and the family moved him into the same facility. However, because they both have profound disabilities, interacting mostly meant sitting in the same room in silence. Most of us can only imagine how that must feel, to sit in a room full of strangers and your brother, silent, with no way to interact besides people speaking at you, instead of to you.

Video games changed all of that. He was able to play a racing game with his brother. Zane stabbed the bad guys in the face with his caretakers. His dreams of participating in a medium that so many of us take for granted, using technology, finally came to life.

I keep in touch with him and the facility that we helped that day. Several of the children that I met have passed on, succumbing to the illnesses that they fought so hard against. But Zane continues to race around tracks and leap over bad guys with the mouth controller, eye gaze system, and switches we provided so many months ago. His nurses tell me that his overall quality of life has improved. He doesn't get grumpy or moody anymore. He's able to take out his anger and frustrations of life in the video game world. And he finally did whoop his brother's butt in both a racecar and with a sword—virtually.

You see, Zane is 1 of 1000 stories we have witnessed, each of them touching in their own way; some of them still bring me to tears this day.

AbleGamers isn't a normal company. We didn't start this organization as a business. We simply wanted to help people, people who had experienced things and challenges like Mark, Craig, and I have. As someone with SMA, a terminal illness that will eventually lead to my full paralysis and death, I have gone against the tide for as long as I can remember, holding on to every ability and fiber of muscle in my entire being.

Video games have allowed me to experience things that I never would have otherwise. I've met wonderful friends, people who would do anything for me and who I would do anything for, and in the real world, not just virtually. I've met some wonderful women, a few of whom went beyond the realm of friendship. While not all of them lasted, as not all dating does, two of those chance encounters would lead to nearly three-year relationships. It's impossible to say that I wouldn't have met someone who fell in love with me if it hadn't been for video games, but I think it would've been much harder. Video games allowed people to see me for the real person I am, the Steve that is inside a body that doesn't listen to my commands.

To say that video games have changed my life profoundly is an understatement. I've been privileged to give talks on major stages, make it to the final stages of TEDx, be invited to the White House, compete in robotics competitions, and travel outside of my city and state. I have this wonderful job at AbleGamers. I have met amazing friends for life. And I found love, not once, but twice. Each and every one of these things only happened because of what video games have given me. But were all of these things fairy tales? NO! Of course not! Because that's not the way life works. I've gotten to have all of the ups and downs life has to offer, indirectly or directly, thanks to video games and assistive technology. And for every emotional valley I fell down, it made the peak of the mountains even better.

As cliché as it is, life is about the moments we're given, not the number of minutes we live.

No real words can describe the amount of life video games can breathe into you. The only analogy that I've ever been able to come up with that comes close is to ask you if you remember the first time someone you were in love with said the magical words "I love you." That feeling of life pouring into your body, powering your soul, and creating a memory that will stay with you until you draw your last breath, and perhaps beyond. Imagine if someone said to you the only thing you had to do to give someone else that feeling is come up with a way for them to enter the world of video games.

Well, in that case, you'd probably spend your life doing what we do, too.

CHAPTER 12

Sunset in the Caves

Matthue Roth

A T FIRST IT WAS only spoken of on the blogs. It was not something people took seriously; it sounded like a prank, one of those fake-news posts real news sites run when they think nobody's looking. But more people played, and more people posted, and the forums were alight with it: Himby was gone! Himby, the tiny, pink-faced, pixel-nosed, many-skirted titular avatar of *Himby Hibernates*, a series of belowground adventures, a 2D platform scroller, released last year to minor acclaim and mildly respectable numbers—lots of downloads, not much pickup on the optional paid content.

My company had shrugged it away, no major disaster, written it off as a loss, and gone to work on something new. I should be specific: Tesseract, the game studio I draw for, the puppet masters who pull my strings. I designed Himby, first as concept sketches, later art-directed him into a living, breathing 2D being.

Until he disappeared.

I should be specific: Himby wasn't always gone. Most of the time players would boot up the game, and he'd be there, skirts a-bouncing, ready for you to take him on another run. *Himby Hibernates* was an infinite game, a game with no way to win but almost no way to lose, launching you through cave after cave of gnashing moles, falling rocks, and ice floes. But lately, people were starting their games to find he simply was not there. Same scrolling backgrounds, same bouncing enemies, just no Himby.

Meetings were convened. The public, our public, was displeased. No one was roaring for their money back, since no one'd spent money on our game in the first place. It was deeper than dividends. Our corporate name was on the line. Studios had lived or died based on less. Something had to be done.

We ran our QA department into the ground trying to figure out what was wrong. They found nothing and more nothing. The programmers were likewise confounded. Eventually, we turned to the original whistle-blower, the moment and action every developer most dreads: we logged onto our own forums.

One theory was posited that Himby disappeared only on the weekends. This was disproven fast: that post was published on a Sunday afternoon, and seconds later a number of screenshots were published in reply—there was Himby, bouncing away as normal. People began to log the times and dates of his absences.

Sure enough, they all occurred on weekends. But it was sporadic: he'd be outrunning dragons on someone's iPad in Kansas as he faded from Riga, and then he'd show up in Cambodia, only to vanish simultaneously on three different people's laptops in Perth. Finally—G-d only knows how they noticed this, through some algorithm or by staring at charts or just dumb guesswork—a loosely formed team found that Himby was disappearing from Friday at dusk till Saturday at sunset, in whatever geographic region he happened to be in.

Which was how I found myself sitting across from the co-owners of the studio, three uncannily savvy and business-minded investors with a shared penchant for black clothes and blinkless stares.

The first co-owner arrowed the slant of his eyebrows and lips in my direction.

"Do you know anything about this, Mr. Roth?"

Did I know anything? How could I know anything? I was a creative, not a coder. My art was animation, not addition, how things looked, not the way they worked. It was an open secret around the office that I was not very good at video games in general, and especially not at *Himby Hibernates*. My jumps were ill-timed and incompetent, my running skills insufficiently choppy. It was a slightly less open secret that I'd barely played the game. After my role was done, Himby's looks finalized and his movements bequeathed to the tech team, I barely entered that purple-blue world of falling stalactites and attack worms.

"I don't know how to code," I said. "I wouldn't know where to begin."

The second co-owner pulled out his phone, activated it, and appraised the display, keeping it aimed carefully away from my sight.

"Nonetheless, we'd appreciate if you did head up the investigation personally."

"You mean...because I'm Jewish?" My twitchy fingers instinctively leaped to the skullcap on my head.

"Nobody's accusing you," said the third and final member of the triumvirate in a way that could not have been more accusatory. "All we're asking you to do is ask questions. Poke around. See if there's any reason, be it technical or Mosaic, that Himby is keeping the Jewish Sabbath."

I was between projects. I had no reason to refuse, and no excuse. I ventured outside the quiet sanctity of the art bullpen to the place where the cubicle posters changed from Calvin and Hobbes to xkcd and NASA and made contact with the unfamiliar and alien other half of the company—the tech team.

I approached those alien people whom I'd worked beside for years and never had any reason to talk to. I asked every question I could think of. Did Himby have his own code routines, or was he inextricably bound in each level to the code of his environment and his enemies? Could there be hackers involved? Had the program been tampered with? How did the screen know to keep moving at Himby's pace if there was no Himby? How did the enemies know to keep fighting?

It was a slow, fierce grind. The week seemed to last about a month. Finally it was Friday. I staggered home, made it there just before sunset, and finally managed to light Shabbos candles before tumbling off into a deep, deep sleep.

When I woke, I was outside on a bed of grass, near the edge of a mountain. The cliff was bracketed by a ledge of rock. On the edge of the ledge sat a diminutive figure in flamboyantly colorful skirts. His beard poked out to one side. I could tell by the cut of his hair in the back, the off-center crown on his head, it was Himby.

I pulled myself together and ambled over.

"You never get to see the sky, you know?" he said to me without turning around. "Not when you live underground, anyways."

His voice was deep and croaky, but cheerful, as no-nonsense as a plumber.

"So this is where you come." I was drowning in the amber sun rays. "You run away."

"You would, too, if they made you spend your whole life in a cave. Matter of fact, you already do that, don'tcha?"

I struggled against his snap judgment. I don't know why I felt like I had to dispute that, but I did.

"But I like what I do. I get to make video games. I draw all day and someone pays me for it."

"No matter what you do for work, kid, sooner or later it still becomes work."

I slipped onto the next rock over and I took him in. The silhouette of his beard shone proud and dark against the sky.

"So why do you go back?" I said.

"Ya always got to go back. We need something makin' us keep movin' forward. Ya know what they call people who take a rest forever? Dead. Dead! But it's good to have a rest."

"Yeah," I said. "It's good to have a rest." And then I was close enough to look at him. Eye to eye, the eyes I'd drawn making a close and uncomfortably intimate contact with the eyes I'd drawn them with, I asked him: "So what do I tell my bosses? What do I *do?*"

He blinked at me with those big, perfectly round, world-encompassing eyes. And he said, "I don't flippin' know! Buzz off, it's the Day o' Rest. You're the artist. Me, I'm just the art. This is your beeswax, pal, not mine."

I woke up in a sweat, walked around the entire next day with my brain racing and palms itching. The thoughts and the designs in my head swelled, too big to be contained within my skull, needing to break out. When I left synagogue Saturday night, three stars in the sky and the deflated air of a sheen of special energy gone from the world, the others behind me walked home. I ran.

Do you ever feel inspired to work on something with a full, blind passion the exact moment you no longer *have* to? My workday in the office involves an astonishing amount of social emailing, procrastination, and zoning out. But at home, 11:30 on a Tuesday night, I'll be watching the most visually astonishing music videos and feel uncontrollably motivated to solve the airbrushing vignette that's been troubling me all week.

And now, as soon as Shabbos is out, I'm at my desk, sketching concept art, making, coloring, switching to my computer to digitally render these things before they're even fully down on paper. I rotate to another view, add depth and compression. Rotate, start again.

The skirts are almost the same, the face a little different, but not enough to seriously affect the animation. I even give him a blazing white skullcap.

The tech guys are full of questions, but management is satisfied. I'm in charge of the investigation, and I say it'll solve the problem, so it solves the problem. They'll spend the money to implement. Either it works or they'll fire me. And you can call me crazy, I know I'm crazy, but I'm also pretty sure it'll work.

I present the new character to the entire company at the Monday morning meeting. They're all stone silent as I speak. The triumvirate has only one question: "What's the new guy's name?" they say.

I have to think of it on the spot. I pull at the first word that comes into my head.

"Popey," I say.

There's a few murmurs—some nervous, some laughlike—but overall they seem to be okay with it.

"And you're sure this'll fix the Saturday problem?" one of the developers—not a senior one, but a cocky one—asks.

I don't. I have no idea. All I have is a weird belief, just as weird as all my other weird beliefs.

"Just implement it," I say, and walk out. Feeling the warm fresh feeling of power swim over my skin, feeling so good about myself, in fact, that, for the first time in months, I treat myself to an extra-long lunch. I go outside and everything. I even walk the extra-long walk to the kosher restaurant, where I skip the lunch special and order my favorite thing on the menu, an extra-large portion. I walk back to the office, and I take my time getting there.

They plug the Popey code into the game. They don't do anything with it, just softly embed it at the bottom of the project, tied to each device's internal clock. And I'm nervous. All the next Shabbos, I'm nervous. But it takes. I find this out Saturday night, run home from synagogue to turn on the game, and see if I can glimpse a bit of Popey, and instead am assaulted by dozens of emails of congratulations.

And maybe I'm still dreaming as I fire up Himby—normal, cave-dwelling Himby—but I could swear he's grinning at me. Not only that, but tiny clouds of breath puff as he starts his run, clouds I know I didn't design, as if he's just popped back into the cave from somewhere else, as if he's fresh back in the world, as if he's all huffed up and happy to be there.

CHAPTER 13

Distraction and Reaction

On Allies and Terrible Allydom

Shana T Bryant

CONTENT

As Toni Morrison once put it, "The very serious function of racism is distraction. It keeps you from doing your work. It keeps you explaining, over and over again…[and] there will always be one more thing."[*]

It's 2017, and haven't you read this before? If you're in tech, haven't you *lived* this before? The frequency of our diversity fails has become so run-of-the-mill that I began to immortalize all the flavors of terrible allydom and their search for cookies in comic form. But that's the thing, isn't it? One of the most disheartening truths of all our marginalized tales is how familiar they all are, how they all start to blur into a single shared narrative of experience. One might even go so far as to call the problem *systemic*.

So the tale I've chosen is perhaps ordinary but also increasingly common as folks try to figure out how to do this diversity and inclusion thing.

****

The room was silent, for I don't know how long. Days. Minutes. Truthfully, it was merely a matter of seconds, but when all eyes are on you, time seems to skip a beat or two. I took a deep breath. I'd already chimed in

---

[*] Morrison, T. Black Studies Center Public Dialogue, Part 2. Oregon Public Speakers Collection. May 30, 1975. https://pdxscholar.library.pdx.edu/orspeakers/90/

now, perhaps against better judgment, so I tried not to scan the room of colleagues, managers, and execs waiting for my reply. I was not so eloquent a speaker as the man I was refuting, but after decades of blackness and womanness, some might assume me to be at least somewhat learned in the topic. He had just wrapped up an eloquent row against what he called "calling out." Eloquence is too often a substitute for intellectuality, and this middle-aged white man, short and scruffy hairs on the head and chin, had eloquence down *pat*. Today's topic: The Proper Way to Respond to Racism(TM) if you see it, feel it, hear it, experience it. Racism. Any racism. Blatant or unintended. It seemed a big topic, but he had a simple solution as usual. It seemed something into which he felt he'd put some thought.

"If someone says something…insensitive, the worst thing you could do, the *worst* thing…," he paused, "…would be to call them out in front of everyone. People *love* to see someone get something wrong, and they jump on it. If I was in a meeting with a bunch of people—my friends, my colleagues, executives—on diversity or whatever and you call me out like that, I'm not going to want to listen; I'm going to be mad. I'm going to say, 'Well, they called me out in front of everyone. I'm not interested in this anymore.' We turn people against diversity when we tell them they're doing diversity wrong. And what are they going to do? They're just going to scurry right back down the foxhole."

I sighed. He continued.

"If you want to build trust and gain allies, you can't do that by shaming them." A round of congratulatory "yeahs" and "mmhmms" from around the room. A room that is mostly peopled by colleagues in the same identity bucket as his own. I hoped for someone else to say something. *Anything*. Please don't let that stand. Also, please don't let *me* always have to be the lone dissenter.

I waited days. No, weeks. No, *years*. All in the span of seconds. Silence, affirmation, and acceptance, all. I could see people recording his words to their long-term memory. "Yes, you're right." "Don't confront racists." "Imagine how the racists feel." "Just wait, and wait, and wait." "Racism will just solve itself." Yeah, sure it will.

It was clear no one was going to challenge. Of course not. It wasn't their job to speak up. As one of maaaaaaybe two "diverse" people in the room at any given time, I was tasked with that job, as written in invisible ink at the bottom of my job description.

Job Title: Producer

Qualifications:

- Drive evolution and improvement through data and analytics for projects with $60M+ budgets
- Champion efficient and effective cross-disciplinary team processes and pipelines
- Teach white people how not to be racist

Desired:
Teach white people how not to be racist, and do it *with a smile*~

Boom, like I said, right there in the job description. But this time, this was kind've a trap, wasn't it? I mean, dude had *just* railed against calling people out in front of their peers, and here I was, my hand about to be raised, about to be his example of how this can go so right or so very, very wrong. He was passionate. But I was stubborn, and that stubbornness compelled me to put my hand in the air.

"I'm sorry," I began, "I know you were *just* talking about how it sucks when people get called out in meetings, and…here I am." I paused. "The irony is not lost on me," I added. Yeah, I was uncomfortable. Not with the call-out, mind you, but with the awkwardness of it all. The irony was not lost on any of us. "I agree that sometimes the 'best' time to approach someone isn't always in the moment, but it's dangerous to say we should *never* do that."

"Why?"

"Well, because that kind of stance gives people an out to allow racism and sexism and other –isms to pass before their eyes unchecked."

"—I'm not saying you should *never* confront them, just that doing it in front of everybody is a good way to alienate people who are already on your side."

"And *I'm* saying that an ally who isn't willing to learn and take correction is not a good ally. I mean, listen. Sometimes, *sure*, the 'right' way to approach someone who's said something racist/sexist/etc is to get them one-on-one. But other times, the 'right' way to correct someone or something is right then and there in the moment. That serves a purpose too."

"But then you're just responding from emotion," he interjected. "And it's impossible to have a logical conversation."

"No. Racism…is personal. Sexism is personal. If someone says something that I interpret as sexist or racist, that is a deeply personal moment for me. And you can't decide how someone responds to bigotry. Sometimes the response might be what you interpret as 'measured,' and sometimes it might not be. That's what bigotry does: it strikes to the core of your identity. And disregarding a response as 'too emotional' is just a trap. Any response you get is going to be some level of emotional."

****

I want to take a break here. Not only because dredging up old memories of simplistic thinking is emotionally exhausting, but to talk about *why* it's emotionally exhausting.

"Benefit of the doubt." I'm not sure where the phrasing came from. It's old, I'm sure. Too old. Interestingly old. But its origins aren't so important as understanding why we're so intent on offering this "benefit" *only* to one side of these conflicts, only to racists, sexists, the homophobic, transphobic, and xenophobic of most all shapes and sizes.

There's the unspoken expectation of women, of people of color, of whoever is experiencing some invalid and gross things in their work lives, that they must always give the benefit of the doubt to whoever is offending them. That person clearly didn't mean it. Maybe we're overreacting. Maybe we misheard. Maybe we're just crazy people. It was just a joke. Can't you take a joke? Don't you know that *all* lives matter? And so, we double the load. Take the initial offending remark, manage both your own feelings *and* the feelings of the offender before responding, *if* you respond. And even after all that, be prepared to defend a lifelong lived experience filled with thoughtless asides such as these against those of someone whose off-color comment about Muslims or dating a Black girl or pay gaps *must*-have-been-made-in-jest-or-in-good-faith-or-some-other-excuse-that-means-you-should-just-let-it-go. (Sidebar: Do you know how much we *already* let go? But I digress.)

Back to reality. If you recall, we were discussing emotional responses to bigoted comments.

His retort: "But you have to be able to have a conversation."

Mine: "Why does it always have to be a conversation?" I heard or imagined a series of objecting groans pepper the room. "No, no, really," I argued. "Let's not pretend that *every thoughtless remark* is simply an honest mistake or some kind of a misunderstood sentiment or, worse, *a joke.* 98.7%

of the time, the person who spouts off something racist/sexist/whatever-ist is not 'trying to start a conversation.' They're looking for approval. Dude who calls his coworker a 'bitch' or complains loudly about affirmative action bringing down hiring standards…it's not because they're trying to engage in thoughtful debate."

"Then what good does shaming them even do?"

"I'll tell you what it does. The so-called 'shaming'…who said it's for *them*? Sometimes it's for everyone else in that room. They're the ones who need to hear it as much as, if not more than, Offensive Guy #17."

"I guess I just don't see the point of making them feel bad," he literally shrugged. "Embarrassing them in front of their peers? It just feels like you're trying to punish them."

"I don't know how to tell you this, but telling someone that something they've said was offensive is not the same thing as 'punishing them.' If you do something wrong, you should feel bad. Saying so isn't punishment; that's a lesson you're supposed to learn when you're three."

"Besides," I continued, "it might sound mean, but embarrassment is a powerful motivator. Embarrassment changes behavior."

∗∗∗∗∗∗∗∗∗∗∗∗

The proverbial school bell rang, and just like that, we were out of time. Everyone began to file out in a hurry, as if they themselves had been freed from some kind of detention. I was a bit grateful. It's not that a conversation like this needn't be had. Much to the contrary, this room was filled with people who'd both never had one and who also desperately needed to be on the receiving end of it—well-meaning people, many of whom I'm sure would self-describe as "allies," whatever that word has come to mean.

I gathered my things, thinking that the meeting being over meant our conversation was at its natural end. But there was more he wanted to say. More to ask, more to demand. The conversation moved outside. He shared with me his struggles. Why he thought I was wrong, WRONG, to confront someone in front of the room, why he thought that an emotional response could *never* be a logical response, and how much research he'd been doing on this subject of diversity. How much, you ask?

"I've been talking to people for *three months* about their experiences." The emphasis he put on those words was unearned. A sly smile might have curled my lips, as I held in so many pithy retorts. "I just think that responding emotionally isn't going to encourage people who might already be skittish about race and gender and all that stuff. Responding emotionally is just going to send them scurrying back down the foxhole. I know; I've seen it happen. And me as a cis-jet white man..."

"Cis-*het*," I offered, nonjudgmentally.

"Cis-het," he parroted, "As a cis-*het* white man, I can be objective. I mean, you're so close to these experiences, wouldn't I be better equipped to respond...on your...behalf...when...when...?"

He *must* have seen the look on my face, because he stuttered and stumbled through the end of that sentiment, even though it had seemed fully formed enough when he'd started.

"No, no no no..." was all the response I could initially muster. This was that new old logic. That women, people of color, we're all too emotional to tell our own experiences. Let a white man do it. First time I'd ever encountered it said so explicitly in the wild. But before I responded, someone else piped up.

"No, that's not your job. As a cis-het white male, it's not your job to try to take over a conversation or tell someone else's experiences. It's your job to sit down, shut up, and listen to women, listen to people of color. When they tell you about their experiences, their pain, their struggles, it's not your job to tell them how they could have responded, or how you as a 'logical white male' would have responded. It's your job to listen and to learn, because even if you get good at that, you'll still never ever fully understand the experience of being black or female in this industry." It was a welcome interruption.

****

So why this story? I have countless "*Man explains diversity, woman objects, man re-explains diversity because woman didn't get it the first time*" tales, many with far less charitable endings. But here was the importance of not just allies, but allies who *do the work*. Allies who understand the consequence of listening and learning themselves and who know when it's time for them to be a nonsense sponge and protect and support their marginalized friends. I have many people surrounding me who call themselves "allies." This was the first, perhaps only, time where an ally was more than just a word self-applied.

I don't mind engaging. But each and every time I do, it's with the knowledge that it will cost me...something. Whether it's time or energy, my good mood, or just peace of mind, there's always a sense that I'm paying someone else's mortgage. Truth be told, for people of color, there's very little potential for praise or accolades to be won in this game, only risk. Risk of physical/mental exhaustion, risk of saying the wrong thing, risk of saying the right thing and offending the wrong people. It's 95% downside, so that remaining 5%, whatever it contains, can make it seem *so* not worth the effort, but…

EPILOGUE

I often ask myself why I'm still here.

> *"Self, why the heck are you still here? Don't you have anything better to do? Don't you have better books to read, better stories to tell, better places to go, better people to love?"*

And sure, the answer to all that is a resounding "probably." But truth be told, I can't *not* be here. I've *tried*. And yet the games industry, with all its warts and blemishes and occasional antidiversity *screeds*, where I feel alternately comfortable and uncomfortable, where I both belong and am supremely outside of belonging, is something…I'm not done with yet. It's a place where Science and Art come together to make something that is…neither? Both? Beautiful? And that opportunity for *special* is something that I want other women and people of color and LGBTQIA people to feel and experience and discuss. I want them to contribute and make this something *special* into something *unique*, and I want them to feel what I've felt for an industry that simultaneously shuns us and yet can't live without us. (I never said it was a healthy relationship.)

CHAPTER 14

First Loves and True Representation

Maurice Broaddus

L IKE MANY WHO FIND themselves in the gaming industry, my love for all things gaming goes way back into my past and is part of who I am. I ran my first *Dungeons & Dragons* campaign in middle school ... where I was the lone Black guy in my gamer group. I played my first game of *Magic: The Gathering* when I was in college ... where I was the lone Black guy in my gamer group. After establishing my writing career with novels and short stories I landed my first gaming work for Margaret Weis Productions. I first bumped into them at GenCon ... where I was the lone Black guy in the room. I first wrote for their *Leverage* role-playing game and went on to help write both their *Marvel Super Heroes* and *Firefly* role-playing games. It was my geek dream come true.

Then I got the call.

A friend of mine worked for Ubisoft, a Canadian AAA game producer. He was calling to lay out an opportunity for me. He was the lead writer for a game they were working on, *Watch Dogs 2* (this came out a little later in the conversation as NDAs and such needed to be signed first). He headed an all-white writing team, some of whom I knew, and the game they were working on featured a Black lead character (Marcus Holloway). My friend went on to describe the premise of the game. Then he began the delicate dancing-on-egg-shells bit of the conversation. Mind you, I already figured out what he wanted to ask, but I decided to string out the moment and delighted in the awkwardness of it. Look, conversations about race are usually fraught, and I appreciated the chance to not be doing the bulk of the emotional work of it for a change. But the long and short of the request was that they wanted to make sure they got the Black guy right.

What impressed me about their ask wasn't just that they recognized their need but also that apparently they weren't satisfied with just having "representation" but were also interested in doing it right. On my end, the chance to consult on an AAA game? I would have done that for a ham sandwich. Though as a full-time freelance writer, I'd never tell them that.

[On a side note: I had an interesting conversation with a manager at Ubisoft. While we were negotiating my pay rates, she shared the opinion that American writers had been conditioned to work for pennies and be grateful. But Canadians saw writers as having a particular skill set and an expertise that employers were willing to pay for. That expertise she was talking about came into play with the tight turnaround times for the script work.]

At this stage in the development of the game, all teams were essentially working at the same time. Everything from facial recognition/image capture to voice over work was in the process of being completed so I had a small window to work within. Even the writers were working up to the deadline, so I would receive the script in sections. I'd have a couple-day window to go through the scripts, make notes on scenes, rewrite as needed, and send in my suggested revisions. My notes varied, from differing takes on character interactions to language use of characters. It wasn't a series of criticisms but rather a matter of noting potential red flags and notes on how to fix or improve the scene.

The scene I was particularly proud of involved the two Black characters, Marcus Holloway and Horatio Carlin, walking into Horatio's mostly white work place. It involved the characters code-switching when other characters were around and dealing with the microaggressions of their colleagues: an everyday reality for many of us, the little things that most people might not even notice, but it meant the world to me to see it play out. That was the real key.

Once I finished the work—made my suggestions, turned to the notes, voiced my concerns—they listened. Ubisoft didn't just check off the box for hiring a consultant and then move on. What could be changed, given the parameters, was changed. Don't get me wrong, the writing team was over 80% of the way "there" in terms of getting the characters and scenarios right. By many teams' measure, that would have been good enough. However, the level of writing of a game is important. It wouldn't matter if the game was 95% of the way there if the 5% took a player out of the game. I'm not saying that we got it 100%, but I was brought in to address problematic moments, add nuance, and add another layer of verisimilitude to the gaming experience.

These days I'm working with a group of community organizers. There is a team within the group, a group of young Black men, putting together  a gaming tournament for the neighborhood. To look at them, some might write them off as thugs. But real recognizes real, and we see each other as nerds in the hood. We simply want to see ourselves—portrayed well and true—in the things we love. And we love to play games.

CHAPTER 15

Overcoming the Unicorns

Normalizing the "Other" in the Games Industry

JC Lau

CONTENTS

For most of my life I have defined myself as an "other": I am the child of Chinese migrants who grew up in a Western-style culture. I grew up in a predominantly non-English-speaking household until my family moved to Australia in the early 1980s, and I learned the language of my peers. I started gaming when I was three: my parents—my mother especially—saw the value of learning how to use a computer early on, and my first game was *Pac-Man* on an old Apple IIe. By the time I entered the games industry in 2016, I'd experienced a lifetime of othering. Why would I enter an industry that's reputed to be full of straight white men? What would possess me to work in an environment where, on a daily basis, I would be made aware of how different I am from most of my coworkers?

The short answer is: because I love games, and I believe that we deserve better than the current state of the industry.

BEING AN "OTHER"

I was seven when my otherness was first used against me. In music class, I was grouped with two white girls to fill out our workbooks. I don't recall how it started, but I clearly remember that at one point, one of the girls called me a "Chinese gong." I was confused—or maybe I didn't want to believe what she had said—after all, we were in music class. And then the other girl repeated it. And then both of them chanted and pointed and giggled like it was hilarious. I don't even remember their names, but I do remember how I felt. I remember smiling and pretending to laugh along while fighting back tears. I remember that I went to the teacher, not to tell her what had happened, but just to let her know that I had trouble with my assignment and could she be my work partner, please? I didn't tell my mother about it when she picked me up after school.

Despite my love of games, they were never considered a "real" job in my family. There were expectations. I entered law school, received a law degree, and became a lawyer. Later, I went to grad school, received a doctorate, and became a college professor. It was during grad school when my department assigned me to teach a course on race and gender issues in America. I dryly commented to the department head that as the only nonwhite, nonmale, non-American in the department, I was probably given this course so I could tell everyone (in a college town where Asians made up less than 3% of the population) what was wrong with society. He didn't respond.

Why am I telling you this? My experiences are littered with stories like these, where (intentionally or not) I am made to feel different, or foreign, or that I didn't fit into whatever the relevant social groupings are at the time. The time I was described as "that oriental girl" at a roller derby tournament by the opposing team. The time nobody wanted to spar with me in kickboxing class because I was the only woman. The times I've spent at conferences, surrounded by a sea of white, male faces. The many times I get asked where I'm from, and when I say I'm Australian, I get complimented on my ability to speak English.

Human beings are complex and highly intelligent creatures, and one product of our ability to process a lot of information quickly is that we end up generalizing and categorizing things. Studies, for example, have shown that children can begin to acquire race and gender categories and stereotypes by the age of 2.[1] However, it's *how* we apply these categories that can be problematic.[2]

WHAT IS IT LIKE TO BE A UNICORN?

When I was 34, I changed careers and entered the games industry. I would often joke that I had traded in the old white men of college administration and tenure tracks for the younger white men of startups, technology, and digital entertainment. Even though the careers were quite different, the cultures were not. The politics are the same. The othering is the same.

I work in test, a discipline where, again, stereotypes abound. Test is often perceived to be the lowest and most expendable part of the industry, where ideas of crunch, poor hygiene, and low expectations persist. My parents—so proud of their doctor-lawyer-professor daughter—were unfamiliar with the disciplines within the games industry and were probably quite disappointed that I didn't persist in a "prestigious" career (although they won't tell me that to my face). That said, some of my cohorts are brilliant coders, designers, and artists who *chose* to go into test. People are often surprised when I tell them that I have a doctorate and I test video games.

But skills from academia transferred over surprisingly neatly into my new line of work. Being able to communicate clearly for logging a bug is effectively the same as being able to take a lot of dense information and process it in a way that makes it digestible to someone unfamiliar with the subject—something that teaching taught me. Having skills for project management and juggling tasks (such as from the academic trifecta of teaching, publishing, and administration) translated to my ability to scrum master a team. Copious amounts of writing experience have made me well suited to producing technical documentation for the studio. And my background and experiences in being an other also has played a part in how I contribute to my studio's culture.

Once I was featured on a podcast on women in games where I was described as "a unicorn": the uncommon state of being a queer woman of

---

[1] Phyllis A. Katz and Jennifer A. Kofkin, "Race, gender, and young children," in Suniya S. Lutha, Jacob a. Burack, Dante Chicchetti, and John R. Weisz, *Developmental Psychopathology: Perspectives on Adjustment, Risk, and Disorder* (Cambridge University Press, New York, NY, 1997), pp. 51–52.

[2] See, for example, Harvard University's Implicit Bias Project, which is a series of online association tests you can take to examine your biases across a variety of verticals, such as race, gender, or class.

color in the games industry. I think it was intended to be a compliment. Unicorns are, at best, rare: I work in a studio of over 600 people, and, of my coworkers, I'm not aware of anyone else that occupies that particular trifecta. (Of course, there are many other equally uncommon ways to be an other, and there are just as many combinations of otherness. There may be other *types* of unicorn, to be sure.)

But here's the thing. Being a unicorn—regardless of the parts of your identity that make you get described as such—is neither intentional nor desired. It's tiring and isolating. I am a unicorn for being a queer woman of color in the games industry—a place historically designed so I do not fit in. I am a unicorn because people use the word "despite" to describe my achievements, rather than refer to my actual talents: *despite* the challenges of the industry's sexism and racism, I have somehow managed to get my foot in the door. I am a unicorn because I exercise absurd amounts of emotional labor daily, from impostor syndrome to tolerating mansplaining and whitesplaining from even the best-intentioned of coworkers. I am a unicorn simply because I am an "other."

CARVING OUT SPACES

I like to imagine that there is some possible world where having 600 homogenous straight white men in the same workspace might be logistically preferable from a human resources or conflict avoidance point of view, but we do not live in that world. To be clear, I am not trying to say that uniqueness is a bad thing. Being unique, as a result of traits over which you have no control or responsibility (such as your race or gender), is uninteresting and unfair, for two reasons. Firstly, it is unfair because it removes autonomy from the individual holding that trait (in that you have no ownership over those traits: you don't cultivate or develop your race and gender as you would, for example, kindness, athletic ability, or being well-versed in pop culture). Secondly, it is unfair because it means that by happenstance of their birth, individuals enjoy benefits and suffer from disadvantages determined by social norms.[1] Why can we not identify people by other properties—ones that they have chosen for themselves (such as the ones mentioned earlier)?

---

[1] There has been considerable discussion on how to remedy this inequity. See, for example, Ayelet Shachar, *The Birthright Lottery: Citizenship and Global Inequality*, 1st ed. (Harvard University Press, Cambridge, MA, 2009).

So, in our actual world, where people are born with traits that will be used in a workplace of over 600 people—some of whom might not be men, or white, or heterosexual—it is almost a necessity that there be room to carve out space for yourself, whoever you might be. I think that as cultural shifts away from racism and sexism occur on a societal level, they are inevitable in the workplace. I entered the games industry after the events of Gamergate, and the impact of those events are visible in the current cultural evolution I see at work.[1]

At one point, the inside joke at the studio was that there were more men named "Dave" employed than there were women in total. At my interview, I asked members of my (entirely white and male) interview panel what the ratio of men to women working in the studio was. Nobody knew offhand, but some did make efforts to find out and let me know afterward (the answer was roughly 10:1). It's not a great statistic, but I soon discovered that those women made a virtual space for themselves. To start, there was an online group established to discuss anything from issues of gender equity to the more mundane "hey, I found someone's cell phone in the bathroom." Then there were collective efforts to bring gender issues before leadership, both within the studio and in the game direction. Finally, there were outings organized to see films such as *Wonder Woman*. And, as the women supported each other, interests were shared and voices lifted together. So there was an existing precedent for those spaces.

From what I discovered, my studio only had the women's group for "others" at the time I started. Admittedly, most of the women in the studio are white women, so I wouldn't have expected much more. So I, among others, set about carving out additional spaces as they were needed. I was one of the first members of the LGBTQA* discussion groups at my studio when it was established in 2016, and in 2017 I founded the discussion group for people of color.

The value of having groups where you are not the minority isn't just that there are traits and interests that you share with other members of that group. There's something more subtle there too: you can speak freely, without having to worry if the person you're speaking to truly understands where you're coming from. You can cut through all the setup that you'd

---

[1] Gamergate is often described as the turning point in game development culture, in terms of addressing sexism and gender discrimination: Susan Kelleher, "'This Has Got to Change': Women Game Developers Fight Sexism in Industry," *The Seattle Times*, August 13, 2015, http://www.seattletimes.com/pacific-nw-magazine/game-on-women-are-developing-new-video-games-and-a-new-culture/.

otherwise need to explain to someone who doesn't share that background. For example, speaking to other westernized Asians about the politics of food, or representation in media, or cultural appropriation doesn't require a lengthy exploration of the Asian diaspora. We see each other; we just get it. Having spaces to identify and relate in those ways is important and refreshing.

But that wasn't all. Shortly before I started work there, my studio began conducting a series of internal town hall discussions, which are streamed to all employees. The studio provides an online portal where employees can submit questions (anonymously, if they so wish). They can then upvote questions, and the leadership team answers the highest voted questions in the town hall.

Unknown to me at the time, I asked the first diversity-related question for a town hall, and from there, the conversation snowballed. Incidentally, I was also fortunate enough to have an ally and a patron (however informal) at my studio who connected me to people in studio leadership and HR interested in starting a conversation about diversity at work. From there, I outlined the three main areas where I believed the studio could address diversity and inclusion initiatives: at the studio level, within our gaming community, and across the industry as a whole. After that, I helped facilitate focus groups within the studio on those three verticals, so we could gather feedback from interested parties on how we, collectively, should address diversity issues that mattered to us. Over 150 of my coworkers participated in the pilot program. It was heartening to know that I was not alone.

Using the data we gathered, we established an official Diversity Committee in early 2017, dedicated to improving the standards set for matters of diversity and inclusion in the studio. We wanted to provide a safe haven for employees, and we work regularly to improve our policies and practices to make our studio a safe, respectful, and inclusive workplace. The ambit of the committee's work includes encouraging diverse hiring and outward presentation, supporting underrepresented groups and individuals at outreach events, and keeping the conversation on diversity and inclusion going within our studio and our industry as a whole.

There are times when it feels like an uphill battle, but there are also times when you can see the tide turning.

The studio recently redesigned our website to showcase members of different disciplines (such as design, art, production, test, and localization), and virtually all of those pictures contain faces of different colors and genders. Our leadership team unveiled a set of company values, and diversity and inclusion were specifically among them. In 2017, we took part in our first Pride Parade and our first GeekGirlCon, and in March 2018, we hosted our first diversity-focused panel at the Game Developers Conference in San Francisco.

Paradoxically, I recognize that the more unicorns there are in the games industry, the fewer "unicorns" there actually will be. By normalizing what makes people "other," they're no longer othered. They no longer have to be unicorns, at least with regard to the aspects of their identities that are theirs by birthright.

And, for me, that is a good thing. I would much rather work in a games industry where I am surrounded by a range of people who are dedicated, intelligent, and good at their jobs but who are recognized and known for *those* traits, rather than ones that occurred by accident of birth. Learning about people and the stories about the paths they have chosen, lifting underrepresented voices, sharing experiences and viewpoints to make great game content, and creating accessible, welcoming, and inclusive spaces for people who have historically been othered—*those* are the reasons I work in games.

The Token Trap

Elizabeth LaPensée

CONTENTS

B EWARE OF FALLING INTO the Token Trap. In the context of games, tokens represent your efforts in collecting and accomplishing tasks and trading them to earn advantages. As a developer, a token is what you become if you let yourself be used to singularly symbolize a particular community. Along the way, there will be traps that you can avoid and dismantle.

THE "FIRST EVER" TRAP

It does no good to let the media say that either your work or you are the first ever unless you're absolutely sure it's true. Even then, it is important to acknowledge how you got to where you're at and who played a part in making that path possible.

The media is largely culpable for this trap since they usually won't cover a story unless it qualifies as "new" by their definition. However, it doesn't benefit your communities to continue to distance them from the perception that they are capable and present in game development.

Instead of allowing yourself to be positioned as the first, be very specific about what is unique about your work while also naming those who influenced you and came before you. Your work is important because your voice is important, and that's all there needs to be.

THE "BOX" TRAP

Ideally, you should be seen as a game developer who can make any kind of game you want to because of your skills. Unfortunately, people will want to define you and thus pin you into only being able to create certain kinds of games. This can mean they think all of your work has to represent the culture or your community in a very particular way. Of course, this thinking often goes hand in hand with presuming culture or community has to be conveyed in a way that is understandable and interesting through their lens.

When you defy those false boundaries and binaries, people will resist and think you are contradicting yourself. Remember, this is about definitions and categories. All along the way, it will be up to you to make corrections of clarification and be clear that there are many ways people can express themselves through game development.

Always define yourself for yourself by writing your own articles and giving clear talks to offset interviews and assumptions.

THE "ONLY ONE" TRAP

Assumptions will be made that you are in some way special and different from the rest of your community members because of where you're at in life. Education, access to technology, and your very ability to use technology can be turned into qualities to other you from your communities. It's great to have your work leveraged and given attention, but not at the expense of how your communities are perceived.

Break the cycle of stereotyping by naming other game developers from your communities and their work. If few people from your communities are working in game industry, turn the conversation to such issues as the lack of access to technology and then quickly move on to solutions. Discuss ways people can help, such as providing workshops, hosting game jams, and donating equipment and services to communities.

Emphasize how you were able to develop games and who has been involved in that work as well as how people can contribute to building capacity for communities to express themselves through games in any way that is best for them.

THE "VOICE" TRAP

Opportunities will come up that put you in a position where you are asked to speak on behalf of all of your community and even loosely related communities. You may be offered gigs where you are expected to voice your approval on behalf of a community or you may be interviewed in ways that position you as an authority.

Watch out for being used. Stay on top of how questions are worded during interviews and talks. Be very mindful of what roles people want you to fill and who actually benefits from using your name as a stamp of approval.

Always speak from your own experiences and not "for" other people. Get to know and be able to recommend other game developers who may be a better fit for a particular game, as long as they won't be in a position of being used.

THE "MISUSE" TRAP

Although it's certainly not on you when your voice is reworked, it's something you need to watch for and correct. Most often, media and scholars will paraphrase you or even misquote you in articles and talks to fit their own perceptions. However, this can completely change the intended meaning or at least adjust it in such a way that it is not true to you and your communities.

When you catch a reworking, don't just let it slide, because this work will be seen by others, and perspectives will be affected. It's easy to feel that it's enough to share the article and comment on social media about what changes need to be made. However, not everyone out there is going to be connected to you and be able to access this important information.

As rough as it is, you need to go to the source and set them right. Whatever the writer tells you, articles can be edited, editors can be contacted, and your support network can get involved if needed.

Stand up for yourself and do all that you can to make sure your voice echoes through the generations in the most genuine way possible.

THE "SAFE CHOICE" TRAP

Be mindful of how you are seen by people and watch out for the nuances of privilege even when you are considered diverse within the game industry. Unfortunately, events tend to pick speakers with lighter skin tones who can represent communities to check off on their diversity checklist.

If people keep coming to you with speaker requests even when there are accomplished peers living closer to that venue who are not as light as you are, call it out. Suggest other speakers whose voices have been marginalized or even silenced entirely. See how the venue responds and watch for if they are accepting or if they insist on you being the only option because it is your image they feel comfortable with. If they keep pushing, just don't go, because the least you can do is not be the one who gives them the ability to check their box.

While tokenism is a constant battle as you level up as a dev, traps can be avoided and dismantled by looking for them and arming yourself by being true to your voice and other devs in your communities.

CHAPTER 17

My Own Damn Game

Jaym Gates

MY FIRST *DUNGEONS & DRAGONS* game was with four industry veterans. Not just guys who had played for years, but guys who had actually developed the game. Nothing like being thrown in at the deep end.

Fortunately, the two running the game were merciful and gave me a chaos-oriented paladin. Our host had mead and scotch for us to go with the usual snacks. It turned out to be handier than he'd perhaps planned. The gamemaster (GM) began drinking heavily about two minutes into the game because one player wouldn't stop punning, one had somehow ended up with a cross-dressing rogue, and I was being myself, which is just never good for anyone trying to run a serious game. We romped through the first half of the adventure, puns and lipstick flying, trying with all our might to break the game master.

And then we were looking at a statue, and the kobold shaman we'd kidnapped was telling us we needed the relic the statue was holding. Since I had the most health, I was obviously the one who would find out if the statue was cursed. Since it had been decided that I should hold the prisoner (after he utterly failed to escape), I said, "Well, I grab the kobold and stick him in the water to see if it's cursed."

The GM had been getting in character for the non-player characters (NPCs), but at this, he stopped, looked at me in horror, and said, "Why would you DO that?" as if I'd suggested using one of the player characters as a mine sniffer. He took a drink to stiffen his spine and enacted a drowning kobold, assuring us that the water wasn't booby-trapped. So, I stepped in and reached for the statue.

The bastard fried me, in my heavy metal plate armor, for about half of my remaining health. His smug rebuttal was that, although the water wasn't cursed, the statue was.

And thus, when the question of "What do we do with our prisoner?" arose, I stuck him face first in the fountain and left him to drown for real.

At the end of the game, I took all of the special powers and skills I'd been sitting on and unleashed them on the undead horde, arranged so that they would build on each other to simply crush the enemy. The battle ended before the GM even got to reveal all of his deviltry. I'd figured out how the game worked and had already started subverting the system with far too much glee. But that wasn't really what I took away from the game.

It is emotionally painful for me to make a mistake. I know *why*, I know the psychological damage that led to it, but that's not helpful in handling it. It means I overthink the simplest things. Most people learn to play as children. I did not. I grew up very fast and was running a ten-horse ranch by the time I was twelve. By fifteen, I was managing that ranch, working for a trainer about an hour away, working part-time as an office assistant for my grandfather's engineering firm, and homeschooling myself. Play was a luxury I didn't get to indulge in.

Now, as an adult, I do, but it's hard. It feels childish and wasteful. I also worry that I'm not doing it right. Drowning an NPC just because sounds awful—and yet. It was playful, and silly, and oh did I pay for it, and oh did we laugh. Colleagues I respected and liked were laughing with me, enjoying the silliness. It was cathartic and wonderful and one of the highlights of my life.

****

I found my way to gaming through an anime role-playing game (RPG). Yeah, I know, but we all had to start somewhere. I don't know how I ended up with the anime geek group, but they latched on to me my first year of college. A few months in, they asked me to play the villain in their anime-based RPG.

I spent hours developing that character. I'd been writing for years, but my characters had always existed within a closed system. When I played with this group, the story was taken out of my hands, and my character had to respond to the story as it was chosen for him. Since it was a play-by-email game, it was the perfect mix of narrative and reaction to teach me how to start thinking about organic characters.

It was also based on an existing character, although not one that was entirely fleshed out, forcing me to be creative within a boundary. Instead of having to build the house from scratch, I just had to supply the finishing details like sheet rock, wallpaper, and furniture.

I had a tendency to write my characters like puppets, mannequins moved by outside strings, with no particular focus or will. They were flat and slippery. Because I couldn't get into their heads, they never became anything more. Eventually, I realized that it was largely because they were all cut from the same cloth, with wildly varying fears and desires pasted slap-dash onto them in an attempt to force them to be unique.

Gaming taught me to create a character from the inside, self-willed and independent of my own needs.

Later, I was a GM for a couple of forums, building stories and developing characters alongside the players. I created a couple of stock characters that I used for most of these, because the familiar characters let me focus more on the other players while using mine as needed to guide the story.

I was going through a rough spell then, having just broken out of a serious relationship with someone who was becoming unbalanced and unsafe. I had also just disowned part of my family after a holiday spent listening to racist rants and enduring abuse from a misogynistic cousin.

I was also dealing with the baggage of a rough upbringing. I grew up in the fringe of an already outlying religious group, in a small town in the backwoods of Northern California. I was also raised by my grandparents, who brought even more old-fashioned beliefs into the mix. The expectation was that I would go to a denominational college, get a degree in nursing, teaching, or related field, find a good husband, settle down, and be a homemaker. I was taught that I had to constantly guard against tempting men to hurt me or assault me.

I was also the youngest in a family of hot-headed, opinionated people. Due to religious beliefs and an unstable home life, I was pulled in and out of the local private school, barely skating through with low grades and high test scores. In sixth grade, I was pulled out for good and lived in relative isolation until I was eighteen. My only social outlet was church, and even that was heavily controlled. We lived about thirty minutes out of town, so I didn't even have people around me in that respect. The only thing I had was the fantasy and science fiction books I managed to buy at the store and sneak out to the barn.

I moved out when I was eighteen, and moved in with my mom, an absolute wreck. No high school diploma, no friends, no social experience, no work experience, not even a driver's license. I took my college entrance exams, got a job, and set about recreating myself. By the end of the school year, I was invited to be on the Dean's List and in an honor society and was doing well at work. I had friends.

The specter of my upbringing wouldn't let go. Just walking into work was physically painful. Walking into a new situation set my stomach churning and put me in a panic. My mom and I both needed distance from family, so we moved to North Carolina, where I would begin putting together a player character: myself.

Gaming was a way to distance myself from the problems and get a bit of outside perspective. My characters could be going through a totally different issue, and because I was focused on that and not staring directly at the problem, the answer would start forming at the edge of my vision.

It also taught me my single most valuable lesson about life.

Most of us seem to be taught that we're little cogs in a grand machine. In a sense, that's true: We are only one part of a big picture. But gaming gave me the framework to see that there's also a little picture, one that I control. I choose where to go and how to get there, what I do when I get there.

My life is a story—one that is prone to look like a surrealist tragicomedy—with all of its own little pieces. But who's writing it? I'm agnostic, so I don't believe that there's a higher being in control of it. So then who? I finally realized that the answer was everyone but me. That had to change.

Once I went to a reading where three authors told a story, made up on the spot, based on input from the audience and each other. The results are easily imagined, I'm sure. Three people, and the story was crazy. How many people did I come into contact with in a year? Hundreds? Thousands? Even if only half of them influenced my life, that was still ridiculous.

No wonder it looked like Mad Libs gone wrong.

Growing up without any sense of empowerment, self-worth, or identity meant that I had two choices: continue to be a nonentity or create myself as everything I'd ever wanted to be. I chose the latter, but I still lacked empowerment. It was only recently that I realized that I'd marginalized myself.

Things happened to me, they would always happen to me, and I just had to accept that and hope for the best. Anything I did would probably meet with failure because I didn't have the power to make any sort of difference.

I made a decision, recently, to stop being an NPC in my own game (life).

Things happen to me, right? No. I happen to things. I'm not the NPC, I'm the GM.

A good GM will take the pieces of a world and assemble them into something fun, well-paced, and engaging. They will work with the players to make sure everyone is having their needs met, resolve interplayer issues, and manage the challenges that arise during play. It's less about manipulation or forcing your will onto someone else than it is about making the best of what you have and being flexible.

It isn't easy. Life throws some pretty wild stuff at all of us, and I seem to be a magnet for strange events and stranger timing. Staying in control of my story means identifying, acknowledging, and choosing a course for every event that comes along. It means jumping off an awful lot of cliffs, too, and hoping that my parachute opens before I hit the bottom.

It means not regretting the mistakes I make, something that I particularly struggle with.

Breaking up with my ex after he became emotionally abusive was one of the hardest things I've ever done. I regretted it for years, wallowing in the guilt to the point of not dating for two years to punish myself for breaking his heart. Last year, I saw him for the first time since the breakup, and we reconciled. I was finally able to look at him again and see all of the things that I'd seen then, and I knew that I'd made the right choice.

It's been a long road. I've told all of these stories before, but each time I tell them, I find a new angle on them, a new piece of the puzzle, a new subplot.

People frequently tell me that they're waiting for that big reveal where we find out that I'm just the construct of an author's imagination.

I am. I'm the construction of my own imagination. Everything I've been through has shaped me, but it isn't the entirety of me. I am my own character, my own person, my own choice.

Life is the sourcebook, the rules, the assortment of premade characters.

I'm the GM of my own adventure, and I'm damn well going to run my own story.

Second Acts

Michael Annetta

CONTENTS

I N HIS FINAL, UNFINISHED, novel, *The Last Tycoon*, F. Scott Fitzgerald famously wrote, "There are no second acts in American lives."* For years, scholars have debated what Fitzgerald meant by this, but I have always read Fitzgerald's quote (as have many others) with a two-act structure in mind: that American lives don't have a restart button, a chance to begin again and continue on through life. In reading the quote this way, I have made a very conscious decision to completely defy Fitzgerald and attempt my own second act. Here is my story, with some advice for those who might want to follow and consider their own second acts.

ACT ONE

I entered the games industry as a second career. While I have always loved games, I didn't consider them as a possible career path until a bit later in life. Growing up working-class poor in rural Pennsylvania, the common directive and advice my siblings and I were given by my parents was "get out." We were the first members of our family (including our extended family) to attend college after high school, and we knew from an early

---

* *The Last Tycoon*, "Hollywood, ETC.," ed. Edmund Wilson. 1941. https://en.wikiquote.org/wiki/F._Scott_Fitzgerald

age that higher education was our key to a better life. I worked hard academically because I knew that a scholarship would be the best way for my family to afford "getting out." But for me, a closeted gay teen, "getting out" also meant much more. It meant not getting trapped in a rural setting where I couldn't be myself or hope to live an open, fulfilling life. With that hope, I started college pursuing a degree in computer science. It was, after all, the 1980s, and computers were "the future." If you truly wanted to be successful and get out, learning about computers was a fantastic option. I graduated at the top of my high school class, and I had already been programming on my Commodore 64 (purchased with money saved up from my paper route) for several years. It seemed to be my best, most sensible path to a bright career.

But I had another dream that kept calling me. I loved the arts. I loved acting and singing and writing and painting and crafting. And despite the legitimate fact that a career in computer science would lead to a more stable and lucrative future for seventeen-year-old me, before my freshman year of college was complete, I decided to shift my focus. On top of that, I was, quite frankly, bored with and uninspired by my major. My future in computers seemed to be headed to a cubicle or clean room, with me wearing a white lab coat and pocket protector. There was no room for self-expression, and for a teenager who was just coming to terms with his sexuality and orientation, I needed to find a better outlet for what I described, at the time, as my "creative side."

I changed my major from Computer Science to Film & Communications. In defending this choice, I actually said, dismissively, to a professor, "I'm too *creative* for computer science. What am I going to do with my life? Make video games?!" And at the time, the late 80 s going into the early 90 s, after the decline of major video arcades and the home video game console market, that made absolute logical sense to me. The original Nintendo Entertainment System (NES) was just starting to catch on in the United States but was still seen as somewhat of an import device, not something that could support or reinvigorate an American industry. Besides, video games were considered frivolous—they were *toys*—not something that one seriously aspired to study or create. No, I would get out by getting creative.

My shift of undergraduate major to film led to my taking acting classes and performing in shows in college, which eventually led to a desire to work more in front of the camera than behind it. After college, I moved to

New York City to study at the National Shakespeare Conservatory, which launched my first career in earnest. I had an exciting and creative life in the theater. I performed in and managed national tours, developed new works, produced, directed, and wrote for and became an active member of several theater companies in New York, Chicago, and Los Angeles.

More and more, I was working with companies that were developing new plays and new musicals, and I was loving the challenge of creating new work. "Storyteller" is a broad and often overused term, but for where I was at that point in my career, it seems most appropriate. I was enjoying seeing how stories could be told across different media and how the rise of the Internet (and that terrible term "new media") kept opening novel opportunities for stories. This curiosity brought me back to work with computers. Once again, I felt the pull of shifting my career focus. I knew it was time for a change and decided the best way to kick start a new career was to return to school.

INTERMEZZO

Returning to school can be a hurdle for anyone, and that hurdle seems to grow exponentially with the length of one's time away from academia. I was concerned with whether or not I could even still compete at a collegiate level. I decided to dip my toes into the waters and began taking classes at a local community college (which I felt was both low cost and low pressure). Somewhat to my surprise, I found out that, yes, not only could I still compete as an older college student, I could excel.

The community college had a very good and well-respected entertainment technology division. I focused on animation, a medium I have always loved but had never really explored much before. My career in theater was clearly an asset, too, since all of my knowledge and experience with character, story, form, and structure carried over into my new studies. Unlike my undergraduate college experience, I was now able to be out and open as a gay man. I was working with fellow students in their early to mid-20 s who treated me like a peer and with whom I could simultaneously learn from and mentor. I was energized, but I knew I needed more of a boost than just a few courses to launch a second career. A good friend, who happened to be a professor at the University of Southern California, thought that a new graduate program in interactive media there might be a good fit. She was right. I applied to the program and took the next step.

ACT TWO

The Master of Fine Arts (MFA) program at USC introduced me to the games industry proper. I had looked at several graduate programs around the country but chose USC because its program allowed students to explore traditional video games as well as other potential applications of interactive media like themed entertainment/location-based entertainment and educational games. I had a large interest in both and obviously wanted to keep my options open for postgrad employment. The department there was actively interested in expanding the diversity of the games and interactive media fields, so being an out gay man was not only comfortable for me, it was an asset. One major difference, though, was my age. About half of my cohort had started grad school right after receiving their bachelor's degrees and were in their early 20s. The other half, save one, were in their mid to late 20s. And there I was, ruining the bell curve at the top.

During our first week of graduate school orientation, I attended a session entitled "Succeeding as a Nontraditional Student." In this case, "nontraditional" was a pleasant euphemism for "older than 25." The session discussed some more typical issues surrounding returning students: how to balance school and home (and employment for those of us still working full-time jobs while attending school), how to adjust your study habits (or regain them if it had been some time since you last attended school), and how to manage the expectations of friends and family members who might not understand *why* you have decided to return to school. A particular point of discussion that was brought up and that has stayed with me all these years is how the transition back to school might force us to leave a portion of our old life behind—how we were crossing a threshold that would change us irrevocably. This was the point that made me feel truly "nontraditional." I had more life experience to draw on from before graduate school, and what I brought with me through that threshold would affect my time there differently than it would my peers.

It was an interesting orientation session in that it was smaller (understandably) than some of the other meetings that week. There were perhaps only about thirty or so people in attendance. We went around the room to introduce ourselves and mention the degree or department into which we were matriculating. A large percentage of the attendees were women between 30 and 50, most of whom happened to be returning to school to get degrees in social work (I have no idea if this was common or just a unique happenstance of the year in which I began), so once again, I was an outlier. Through the group discussion, it seemed that the majority felt that their age and experience would be an asset in their new field of study. When I mentioned that I was studying interactive media and games, I admitted that it was usually a younger person's field and most of the attendees looked at me with a mix of awe and pity. I paused for a moment. Perhaps social work *would* have been the more traditional nontraditional route to take.

Three years of study and work flew by. I honed both my design skills and production skills with internships and professional projects attached to the school. But upon graduating with my MFA, I found myself in a position similar to when I graduated with my BA. It is no surprise that graduates with arts degrees are less likely to find a job right after graduation than, say, business or science majors. For those in the entertainment field, finding work is often a process of activating your personal and professional networks. Internships, friends, professors, and classmates are the best resources for seeking new employment. Though I had cultivated my interest in location-based entertainment and educational games with my work in school, the majority of the job opportunities after graduation were, obviously, still in the field of more traditional gaming. This presented some challenges that have shaped the rest of my career.

In my career, I have focused more on working with indie game development than with AAA development. Primarily, this is because the indie scene tends to create more of the types of games that I personally am interested in. That's not at all to say that I don't love and play AAA games, but I certainly play more indie games. Coming out of school, especially out of a prestigious program like USC's, I was privileged enough to schedule some interviews with AAA developers and publishers.

Nevertheless, interviewing in the AAA world left me feeling uncomfortable and awkward. I wasn't my best self. I would often walk into interviews feeling a pressure to conform, to change who I was to fit the job. Being interviewed by straight men (and it was almost always straight men) made me feel like I needed to go back into the closet (which wasn't an option for me as I have been out professionally for years). What I initially interpreted as a discomfort with my orientation I later came to realize was a discomfort with my age. Why was someone who was older than the interviewer coming in for a junior position? I learned the term "culture fit" quickly and what that might entail. I felt as if I had a "Best if used by..." stamp on my resume. Conversely, when I'd interview with smaller, indie studios, I didn't feel this same sort of pressure. I knew I'd be happier working in those environments, and so I steered my career in that direction.

However, this experience made me consider the possibility that there is an expiration date on *all* developers in the games industry. This is reflected in some other branches of the entertainment industry as well (e.g., screenwriters tend to have a greater challenge after a certain age, though actors might work well into their 90s), but it seems decidedly pronounced in the games industry. In a meeting just the other day, I listened as a veteran of the games industry (white, male, early 60s) talked about a colleague of his who was now moving into academia, saying, "He's gotten to that age where he wants to settle down." Implied in this statement is that prior to a certain expiration date in the games industry, it seems you are expected to be a "free agent." I suppose that means you'll move to a different city if the job demands, or worse, if your job/studio no longer exists and you need to look for a new job, you'll have to expand your search outside of your current geographic area. I suppose that's fine if you're young and single, but if you're slightly older, have a spouse or at least are in a serious relationship (usually with someone who also has their own career to consider), or have a family with kids, how does that then affect your choices and your flexibility? Even if you're advanced in seniority in your career, does that lack of youthful freedom ultimately limit your options? These are questions that still concern me in the games industry.

Another challenge that I have faced (and continue to face in some fashion) has been how to showcase all my previous work experience as being directly applicable to my current work. I think this is particularly common to most people who shift careers, but unlike those fellow students shifting into social work, life or work experience feels less valued in games. Suddenly I'm not someone with a wealth of storytelling and production knowledge; I'm an older person, but one with no relevant experience. To put this into gaming terms, I have high XP, but the save file won't load to the next level.

On the other hand, along with my high experience points, I also happen to have high HP. I was an actor. I learned how to take rejection early on in my first career, and those hit points carried over into my second. I have a resilience that has been honed in ways that some of my peers can't imagine. A bad Steam review for a game? Bah, that's nothing compared to a chilly audience when a joke falls flat. A playtest returns less-than-desired responses? I would rather have that than forgetting my lines in front of a full house. Nervous about pitching to a new client? Couldn't be worse than three auditions in one day in different parts of town. It takes a lot to knock my HP down, and those HP only came with my life experience. It's something I remember every day.

My observations of the gaming industry, both from the inside and from the margins, are that we collectively have a difficult time dealing with age and, by extension, growth. We tend to devalue experience in exchange for novelty. Novelty is, of course, lauded in all branches of the entertainment industry, but other media have learned to expand to accept the new while also retaining their experienced people and the perspective they bring. The games industry often treats its members like citizens in the world of *Logan's Run*—once you're over 30 (or, worse, 40) your usefulness has been depleted. (And, yes, I'm well aware that a reference to *Logan's Run* is most likely lost on younger readers. See the previous paragraph about a joke falling flat. I have the HP. I can take it.)

THE NEXT ACT

Why, you might ask, do I still pursue a career in a field where I sometimes feel marginalized? The simple answer is that I love games. I love play. I love people who play games. I believe in the power of interactive experiences to reach audiences in ways that other media cannot. I love virtual reality as a new and rapidly expanding medium, and I can't wait to see where its growth will take us. Working in VR feels like coming full circle for me as it is closer to theater than it is to any other medium, including games. Creating VR is just creating theater using the tools of game making.

Ultimately, I'm still working in games because I fear what we lose when we devalue our aging workforce or a workforce that joins us from other careers. We lose the potential for new audiences. As a society, we're rapidly approaching a point where even senior citizens grew up playing some sort of video games and where practically everyone has some sort of screen device in their pocket. The term "gamer" (as in "one who plays games") has grown so broad that by now it should have become meaningless in terms of identity and audience. We don't claim personal identities based other media, like novels or film, so why would we do that with games? Sure, some might qualify their love of a medium as part of their identity (we'll sometimes speak of "an avid reader" or a "film buff"), but like reading or watching films, *everyone* plays games. My 79-year-old mother, who couldn't for the life of her understand why it was so important that

I have a ColecoVision in my bedroom when I was a kid, plays games on her smartphone all the time. We are all gamers. The differences lie in how we like to commit to games. When I was a teen, I had hours to play games (and I did), just like kids and teens today. But as I got older and had other responsibilities, the sessions of game playing got shorter by necessity. I'm not alone in this. I'm part of a growing, potential audience for different forms of games, and I want to make sure that others see that, too.

Additionally, by allowing more people to cross over into games from other careers, we also introduce new practices. We're already seeing this in the world of VR as filmmakers and musicians are experimenting with this new form and bringing their practices into creating something that is wholly new. I have found it exhilarating to work with people from television and film as they enter the gaming and VR realms to figure out new ways of producing and creating new narrative (and often nonnarrative) content.

Finally, my greatest fear of what might be lost if we devalue an aging or shifting workforce has to do with new perspectives. Too often, I've seen games industry people frame their work only in reference to earlier games. This has the potential of creating repetitive, reductive work leaving us with repetitive, reductive games. Where's the novelty in that? Rarely do I see someone suggest how new work is influenced by opera or jazz or French cuisine or mining or any number of other careers, occupations, and media that could invigorate and shift what we mean when we speak of "games." "New perspectives" doesn't always mean "young" perspectives, and novelty doesn't have to completely reinvent the wheel. Diversity in games can come in many forms and regardless of our gender, orientation, race, ability, or religion, the one human condition that everyone in the games industry *will* experience and no one will ever escape is getting older. We should recognize that, value that, and plan for that.

CHAPTER 19

Firmly Rooted and Ain't Goin' Nowhere

Freelancing While WOC

Toiya Kristen Finley

CONTENTS

I'm Gonna Be a Game Designer, Narrative Designer, and Game Writer!

B ACK IN 2002, I was playing *Shenmue II*. I'd been kicking around an idea for a video game for a while. *Shenmue II* proved that it wasn't far-fetched. All of the locations I saw in my head, the variety of things players could do, the characters players could interact with, the storyline—technology could support it. I was finishing up a doctorate in literature and creative writing at the time. It would be a while before I had the drive to pursue working in games.

Six years later, I made the trek to the Game Developers Conference (GDC). All I knew was that I wanted to be a game writer. I had no idea what to expect. I knew absolutely nothing about game development. Okay, I knew programmers were a thing, but nothing else.

I bought the cheapest pass I could, stayed at one of the cheapest hotels I could find in the area (not that cheap; this was San Francisco). The first day of GDC I carried 50 copies of my CV into the section with all of the

HR people. A thirtysomething, I mixed in well enough with the students and just-graduateds. I waited in long lines at the Blizzard booth. I avoided crowds by finding that lone rep at the tiny stall at the end of the row at the back of the hall. The swag impressed me. I got my fill of T-shirts and pens and light-up doodads.

What I didn't get was a gig.

It's not that I thought it would be easy—the life of the freelance hustle never is. But the HR people had an interesting mix of reactions from "Yeah, we don't need game writers" to "Oh, so *you're* a game writer? I've never *seen* one of *you* before!" Perhaps my recollection is a little unfair, but it certainly felt that way. Studios used in-house writers. Or they had a recruiter find them. Or they had no idea whether the developer needed writers or not. They were all as helpful as they could be and tried to point me in the direction of someone more knowledgeable. Still, I couldn't believe that so few studios worked with writers.

Part of the problem was that I had game writers confused with game designers. (You can laugh.) The other part was that story in games was not as important as it was going to become. I went back home dismayed but still determined. I searched for game-writing work the same way I did my other freelancing gigs: Google searches.

By the next year, and my second year at GDC, I'd found a freelance gig writing lore for Black Chicken Studios, an indie startup. They liked my work and trained me to be an assistant designer on the project. And that's when I discovered there was such a thing as a game designer. As I made my rounds talking to HR reps, they took more interest in me. There were a couple of writing jobs, too.

This time, however, I was dismayed for another reason. They weren't freelancer friendly, and they certainly weren't open to telecommuters. Freelancers, in so many euphemistic words, were portrayed as outsiders. It would be difficult to work with them. Writers needed to be in-house. I understood their reasoning; it was easier to communicate with someone who was *right there*. Someone everyone could talk to face to face without the hurdle of waiting to reach them by email or chat. While I understood, I was frustrated. As a telecommuter, I knew how easy it was to communicate with a client and build chemistry with the rest of the people on the project. It was easy because I had developed those freelancing skills for eight years.

But what I couldn't understand was a question, a suggestion, a piece of advice I got from individuals in positions to hire and employed developers alike: "Would you consider moving to a hub?"

I needed to be in a city where there were lots of studios, where I could bang studio doors when I was looking for work, where I could be in-house. They may as well have asked me, "Are you willing to relocate to [PLEASE INSERT CITY WITH RIDICULOUS COST OF LIVING HERE]?"

"Hell naw!"

Well, that's what I thought. Instead, I gave them a polite translation: "I'll have to talk to my family about it."

But it was a visceral response to this idea that I would have to uproot myself, leave my life behind, and go to a place where I'd have to start over and *hope* to find work. There was an underlying notion of "this is what you must do if you're really serious about making it." Move to a place like San Francisco? Seattle? Without an actual job or my new employer paying for the relocation? Was that possible? Was this a thing people did? To me, the concept was bizarre.

Not to everyone, though. In the years since I'd started working in the industry, I'd seen Facebook posts and tweets from friends announcing they were moving. They would give themselves six months, a year, or some other predetermined amount of time to find work. If they didn't find any, they'd move back home. I wished them well, but I still felt a disconnect with the whole idea. It wasn't until recently that I understood why. That disconnect was cultural. All of these friends had been White. I'd never seen one person of color announce they were taking that risk. I'm sure it's happened. I'm also sure it's a good deal more rare.

Uprooting is expensive. It's not something everyone can do, and many people of color, whether they're just out of school or employed for several years, are not going to be able to cover moving costs, get a place with reasonable rent, or have enough of a cushion in their checking accounts to sustain them for however long it takes to find work.

Nor does moving appeal to them. Community and family—whether that family is biological or by choice—are important to a lot of people of color and marginalized groups. Community is more than a place to belong. It's a joy. It's a source of strength. Community is the people you come back to no matter what you've endured that day. They're there for you, and you're there for them. Asking someone firmly rooted in their community to up and leave would be like asking them to rip out a part of their soul: "You really want to make it in games? Why don't you cleave off part of your identity and move across the country?" That's certainly what it felt like when I was confronted with leaving behind both my biological and church families.

There's only one reason why I'm a freelancer: freedom. I'm an outdoor cat who sometimes plays nicely with indoor cats. The last time I worked in an office, I was getting my doctorate and serving as a writing center tutor. I write and edit for clients, but I also write for myself. Being employed, whether I moved away or stayed in my hometown, would take time and creative energy away from my own projects.

And that freedom has come partly *because* of my family and community. While I was still establishing myself as a freelancer, my mother supported me financially and helped me get to GDC. They may not have understood what my work entailed, but my church family was always happy to pray for me and hear about my successes and frustrations. And you know what? If I had moved, I would have to start all over— in terms of finding not just a new job but a new *community*.

That sounds easy? If you are marginalized, you learn over a lifetime whom you can and can't trust. You can be cool with some friends, but you certainly can't talk to them about some things. I have an internal emotional gauge: there are some conversations I can't have without feeling like I'm being punched in the face … repeatedly. And it doesn't matter if the person I'm talking to agrees with me 100%. It still hurts. If you're not willing to feel like you're being punched in the face when we talk about those things, then don't think I'll be willing to talk to you about them. The psychological cost is too great for me with no sacrifice on your part.

Black folks get emotionally assaulted without warning all the time— law-enforcement shootings where victims are blamed for their own death; harmful, normalized stereotypes appearing in storytelling media and making their way into viral Internet memes; non-Blacks whining about why we're upset and why it's no big deal. Now, imagine me in some new place without "I'll take punches for you" emotional support. I don't know anyone well enough that I feel like I can trust them to discuss how I'm feeling about what just happened. (And, no, sharing on social media doesn't count. Real, lived human connections are still a thing.) I don't know anyone well enough to even *try* to discuss it and see how they will respond, which could be anything from just staring at me to blowing off my concerns to straight up arguing with me.

Yeah … no.

Why would an industry support a culture forcing people to start over if they want to "make it," where they have to learn when they can freely share, when they can truly be themselves, and spend a lot of money with no guaranteed payoff?

So while I might have been hardheaded back then, I was determined to work in games as a telecommuting freelancer. Uprooting my life was not an option.

KNOWING MY WORTH

Freelancing is hard—it has to be said. It's not for everyone. If you have a family, you can't go months without work or income. And if you're an American, you or a family member may need the stability employee benefits provide.

You have to compete to get gigs with a number of qualified, super-talented people. You have to find prospective clients that, ya know, believe *paying* you is actually important. You have to convince those clients that you can help them and that your work—and you—are worth the rates you request.

I've been through lean years as a freelancer. I've walked through "barely making enough" stages of life where I've wondered if I'd be able to cover payments for my student loans. I've wondered, "Will I ever get work again? Will I have to stop pursuing telling my own stories, drop everything, and stop writing and editing altogether?" That may not sound like a big deal, but I strongly believe, now more than ever, that I have stories that need to be told.

Freelancing calls for skills I have to continually strengthen and hone. One thing I had to learn is that it was okay for me to ask for what I was worth, knowing that a prospective client might laugh and walk away. Freelancers tend to undercut themselves when it comes to rates because they're afraid of losing work. But here's the thing: when you ask for better rates, you attract better clients.

The caliber of client I want to work with understands that to get the best, to get the team they really need to make their vision happen, they're going to have to pay for them. They know that quality can carry a high cost. They don't trust freelancers working on the cheap. Getting their attention didn't happen right away, though. I had to work on several projects and extend myself professionally first.

Staying put and continuing to telecommute is what got me greater opportunities. Back when Elance still existed, I had several game-design and game-writing gigs and worked for clients from all over the world. At the same time, because I wasn't anyone's employee, I could travel to conferences.* I was moderating roundtable Q&As for other writers who were looking to get into the industry, leading game-design and narrative-design workshops, and speaking on freelancing. People I met at these events were hearing what I had to say and referring me for jobs.

This might sound like people are getting a little too much up into your business, but you want the good prospective clients, the ones who value you, to vet you. They check out my LinkedIn profile. They read my blog posts. They visit my website. They read through my game design and game writing samples. They look at my CV. In other words, they get to know *me* and whether I'm a good fit for their project. That means they know I've written about race and analyzed portrayals of marginalized people in media. They can read my speaker history and know that I've addressed issues of diversity. They've seen what's important to me because they've read my short stories and character bios featuring diverse characters.

I have dear friends who've gone through very real, terrible discrimination in the games industry and adjacent industries. I've had to deal with jerks and clients who decided they weren't going to pay me (that didn't work out well for them), and maybe prospective clients passed on me because of who I am and what I stand for. But, as far as I'm aware, this is an area of my life where I have not been discriminated against, either as a woman or a person of color. I've wondered why that is. I think part of the reason is that clients get to know who I am before I'm hired for a gig.

As I said, being a freelancer isn't for everyone, for a variety of reasons. However, for marginalized people who might have opportunities to go down that path, I want to encourage them. Someone willing to pay you over $50/hour is going to do it because they believe in *you*. I've gotten over $100/hour on some jobs. No gender pay gap bullshit. No making less because I'm Black. Quality, dedicated clients usually pay for projects that are important to them out of their own pockets, or they have funding from investors who want to make back that investment. They know they need to

---

* I realize this is a privilege I have. While most of what I made a year went into travel costs, a lot of people aren't able to get off from work, or they have dependents and loved ones they can't leave behind.

hire the best team they can. Many of them put together virtual teams who communicate and collaborate remotely. If they believe you're the right person to join that team, they aren't going to reject you because of where you live in the world or who you are.

AN APPEAL

On my seventh consecutive trip to GDC, something strange happened. Veterans in the industry, people I admired, people who'd worked on multimillion-dollar AAA franchises, people who'd helped me understand my responsibilities as a narrative designer, asked me for advice ... about freelancing.

The games industry looked a lot different from when I didn't know the difference between a game writer and game designer. Not only were permanent jobs disappearing, but developers (and nondevelopers) were also looking for freelance writers. There were several reasons for this, but being virtual, a telecommuter, wasn't the negative it once was.

"How do I figure out my rates?"

"What should I have in my contract?"

"How do I define my role with my client?"

I was now firmly rooted and established as a freelance game designer, narrative designer, game writer, and editor. I spent hours in these conversations, covering years of what I'd learned while telecommuting on a variety of projects in different roles. Yes, it does amuse me to think about now versus then.

Years ago, individuals thought they were helping me by saying I had to relocate in order to have a place in the games industry. That same advice today could be disheartening to someone who's looking for their first job. Marginalized people have more opportunities to work in games because development is moving to virtual spaces. While studios still have in-house employees, many are hiring telecommuting freelancers and employees.

I know that it's possible to successfully work in the virtual space. It's time for more developers to explore the value of virtual teams, if not embrace them. I understand why it's helpful to have people in the same office, but there are brilliant people who have the talent to work in games *right now*, but they do not have the financial or emotional means to uproot themselves and look for work.

They should have the opportunity to be firmly rooted, too.

CHAPTER 20

Actualization and Action

Scout Munroe

T HIS ESSAY FOCUSES ON the journey I am on as a content creator with a small channel and the sympathetic shift it inspired in my personal life. The beginning stages were choked with assumptions about my reception and trepidation of being seen as a target, punctuated by moments of battling self-sabotage and attempts to make myself as inoffensive as possible to both new viewers and personal associates. Observation of a culture I had been steeped in gave way to introspection and a momentary flash of spiteful bravery, and when I landed, I found somewhere I could be, comfortably. Where I had once found my marginalizations pitted against each other, accepting that I was experiencing each simultaneously gave me a rare and often silenced perspective that colored my perceptions—whether or not I spoke directly of it on camera. In evaluating my relationship and feelings on my Blackness, my mental illness, and what being Queer means to me, my voice coalesced, and my focus became clear.

The truth is that ThisIsMunroe* was the first attempt at a channel that actually stuck. In about six years, I've made as many attempts to start recording playthroughs, streaming on Twitch, and stockpiling tips and tricks for beginning voice over work. The first inkling I had about wanting to make videos started nearly four years ago with the purchase of an overpowered gaming laptop because I wasn't sure when I would get the

---

* Scout Munroe, ThisIsMunroe, https://www.youtube.com/channel/UC4FJEjNuhu2QHI_Yetl-Zkw (accessed August 13, 2017).

chance to afford another. Overnight, it felt like I had a real computer that was capable of running programs that would make my older one stutter and freeze and allowed for more creative endeavors. Following a good dozen of different creators online, I saw nothing of myself in the voices of the community and very little in the games I played. I took notes, planned an idea, and was sidelined frequently. Sometimes projects were abandoned because of a sudden change in personal circumstances. At other times, I balked at the idea of trying to conform myself to acceptable standards as a nerd and scrubbed all attempts from the Internet.

Sometimes, my mistrust of the gaming community was well founded. Scores of racial slurs would appear in comment sections as companies announced games that deviated from scruffy white dude protagonists, games that would show astounding amounts of sensitivity for survivors of abuse in one breath and turned a transwoman into a joke in the next. People who criticized the work of those who claimed to be allies of the marginalized were told they were overly sensitive. Every voice I heard speak up was shouted down, and for a while, all I could summon in the attempt to say something meaningful was silence.

Despite the fact that groups formed to support those frequently ignored by gaming culture, I found myself wracked with the sort of anxieties born of having to consider how others perceive you. My blackness was always policed by people amazed that I wasn't like "those" Black people or by those who found my queerness unpalatable. I worried I would get booted from groups devoted to empowering women in nerdy spaces once they found out I wasn't a woman. Getting caught up in the optics of gaming, YouTube stoked the flames of impostor syndrome, and trying to obey the confines of my closet only worsened the situation. In my personal life, I enforced boundaries in half-steps—terrified that if I pushed too hard or asked too much, I would be abandoned by people I had grown close to. The anxiety from all of this leeched into every video and audio file I recorded, with dysphoria running rampant as I failed to meet external standards of femininity or my own wishes for self-actualization.

The stress always started internally, rising in intensity when I looked at my peers, and I was so used to what gaming was "supposed" to look like that I minimized my own feelings on the media I was consuming and held the feelings I wanted to express to a much higher standard. I wasn't really losing anything by waiting to make things, right? I would tell myself that who I was didn't matter, so long as I made good content. If I got the follows and the subscribers, what did it matter that people assumed that I was a woman? Moment after moment, the things I had internalized sapped my desire to create and undermined the thoughts and efforts I managed to cobble together. The videos I made reflected this insecurity and got weaker with every attempt, and the projects to practice my acting never materialized. I watched as dark parts of the Internet rose to devour women who spoke a little too loudly and wondered how quickly harassment would start for me—considering that nonbinary was largely considered a word made up by bored, attention-seeking teenage Tumblr users.

Years of frustration coalesced into spite, dry tinder waiting for a spark that came after a move across the country. The first video was posted to share my experience with friends and family, a group of people who always encouraged me to do something with all the ideas that I would get, and, frankly, I got sick of getting clocked for being a procrastinator that ran their mouth a lot. Focusing on just the games I would select for a month and the experience of playing let me pour my restless energy into actual projects. The dysphoria I felt, which I used to only be able to articulate as hating my voice, ebbed when I made videos for the people who already knew who I really was.

I started my channel two days shy of my thirtieth birthday, my mind consumed with the thought "I am tired of waiting." After all, waiting had been something of a lifestyle for me, and while thirty is not old by any stretch of the imagination, the idea of putting off something I thought could help me work toward fulfilling a long-held desire made me uneasy. I spent the first half of my life learning how to navigate the fallout from my abuser's failures. It took me twenty-six years to come out and nearly another four to get comfortable with correcting pronouns. After I finally corrected my legal name, I gained a fleet of new accounts—reborn online as I made a concerted effort to live more authentically. I stopped giving people permission to misgender me, and when I pondered making videos specifically about my gender, I met with resistance. People told me that I was being dramatic, that my deadname—in all its variations— was easier, and I was only coming out for attention. Understanding that sometimes the people who got you through one struggle will fail you in another, I discovered that spite is a damn better motivator than some financial incentives and that making things became easier once I stopped being afraid of being outed. By the time I hit record, I had become someone nearly unrecognizable, failing to notice that all the necessary components for my newly minted voice had started nearly nine months before.

It is taxing work, but as I learn my way around programs and websites, I also learn ways to navigate things I never had words for before. Working to post consistently can agitate the mental balance I have to keep with my bipolar disorder, so sometimes I just roll with it. Bless the Internet, batch recording, and scheduling uploads, bastions for those laid low by depressive swings. I do everything for my channel myself, and by splitting my focus between so many skills—filming, graphic design, video editing, and social media management—I have little time for the maladaptive thinking that formerly prompted mass deletions. No longer do I suffer months of work lost in a single fit of perfectionism. Finally, there are other things to pick at—making sure an audio cue is just right or refreshing so I can make sure to respond to all of the comments on last week's videos.

The words that failed me so frequently before come easier with each post. For the first time, I've had the chance to bond with other players about actually being about to play as a nonbinary pc, and I've had talks about the meaning of memory and what the right action is in a world that is falling apart around you. My channel is small, any way you slice it, but the community I am finding as it grows feels powerful. As time goes on, I want to use my voice to help others find theirs—both literally as an actor and as someone once rendered speechless by my peers, and I would like to have my community join me in that. We're a quiet little section of the Internet, one part of the cacophony of voices in the gaming community—but we are here.

Scout Munroe is a game tester, YouTuber, aspiring voice actor, and long-time lover of games located in San Diego. In their spare time, they enjoy good food and interesting convention panels and can be found just about everywhere on the Internet as "ThisIsMunroe."

CHAPTER 21

When Games Get Political with Me

Joshua Kyle Boykin

N EXON'S RIDERS OF ICARUS felt gorgeous even before I got in-game. Like most MMOs, *Riders of Icarus* had a hook: you could capture, summon, and ride mounted dragons from early in the game. In an open, colorful world, players create their rider in a fantasy world where fire-breathing beasts multiple times your size obey your every command. Excited as I was, I stalled internally at the character creator. When I asked the developers I was on the call with about my issue, they told me there would be multiple "beautification options available for purchase" in the game.

At least this meant that black hair was being described as a "beautification"? That's a positive, right?

Working as a game journalist has its perks, one of them being the chance to play games early. Often during press previews, developers are still building the titles you're playing: terms like "pre-alpha" get thrown around frequently to pardon bugs and glitches. Sometimes the issues in pre-alpha aren't technical errors, though: they're oversights, dev-team blind spots.

When it comes to issues of race, there's no guarantee they'll make the fix list or even emerge as priorities to fix. As a black journalist, I'm more sensitive to portrayals of blackness in games, especially in character creators.

In this case, I wanted my character to have the short-length "natural" haircut Evan Narcisse references in his article "The Natural: The Trouble Portraying Blackness in Video Games."* Portraying blackness seems to spell trouble for many games, and advocating for it can also be tough.

Maybe if I'd been able to find the oversized-afro many character creators slot in to their tools, I'd have stayed quiet. Maybe even if I could have made my character bald. The *Riders of Icarus* meeting was virtual, with a handful of other journalists involved who seemed to have no trouble creating their own characters. But neither bald nor afro was available, just a host of seemingly not-black hairstyles.

And maybe this memory wouldn't have sunk so far into my brain if the developers had said something like the generic "Thanks for that feedback, we'll take it back to our team" often heard during game demos. Instead, the answer felt like, "Oh, we have black hairstyles in the game…you just have to advance far enough to unlock the ability to purchase them." Embarking in the world of *Riders of Icarus* with black hair was a "feature": optional, a cosmetic purchase, a novelty.

Free-to-play as the game may be, I haven't gone back to play *Riders of Icarus* since.

Discussions about portrayals of blackness aren't new: from the angry, vulgar Barrett of *Final Fantasy VII* to Cole Train in *Gears of War* and the Jubilant Catarina in *Dark Souls*, there are plenty of opportunities to talk about blackness in gaming. I always hope that as a journalist I can help make positive changes in newer games by raising my concerns. More often than not, they seem to fall into a responseless void.

At E3 2017 I played *Absolver*, a strategic fighting game developed by Sloclap. Previewing the game in the Devolver Digital trailer, I ran through the 3D world with a member of the art team. When it came time to choose a character class, I had one of three options: the balanced, versatile Forsaken; the punishing, tough Khalt; or the agile, quick-moving Windfall. There were both male and female models for each class, but no chance to customize them further physically. I realized as I flipped through the classes: the jack-of-all-trades Forsaken class seemed white, the dexterous martial artist Windfall seemed Asian, the damage-absorbing, brute-force Khalt was black. Offensive? No. Trope-laden? Yes.

---

* Evan Narcisse, February 13, 2017. *The Natural: The Trouble Portraying Blackness in Video Games.* https://kotaku.com/the-natural-the-trouble-portraying-blackness-in-video-1736504384

Where many trope-y portrays can feel offensive by painting black characters as meatheads (particularly black men), the *Absolver* demo didn't do this. Since Khalt is a fighting style, a class instead of a race, it's possible they'll include a character creator that would make this whole discussion moot. It'd be to the game's benefit to allow character customization; otherwise, characters telegraph their fighting styles by the skin-colored uniforms they wear. But when I delivered the feedback to PR after I'd written up the preview? Silence.

Perhaps where the silence felt most deafening, though, was when I recently played *Final Fantasy XIV*, Square Enix's MMO originally launched in September of 2010. It's received multiple expansions and patches, including a systematic overhaul with the release of *A Realm Reborn*. And yet, this year, while exploring the realm of Western Thanalan in Ul'dah with my new character, I stumbled over a piece of dialogue that tripped me up even more significantly: an Ul'dahnian off-handedly referencing American slavery reparations when describing her own entitlement.

I sometimes feel like people think I bring up issues of race because I'm trying to be obtuse, to so frequently be the one black journalist in the room and say, "Hey, but what about this black people thing?" It's like I can hear a million eyes rolling in unison, feel the voices of ten thousand people saying "Well, *I* thought it was funny" all at once. Those are people I imagine feel like "politics" are being forced into games, that I'm an Agent of PC Culture coming to steamroll media and the world. I imagine those are people who care about games, immerse themselves in them, and are disheartened when that immersion is broken. They're trying to protect that immersion.

In *Final Fantasy XIV* there are plots of land available for purchase in an area called "The Goblet." Imme, a Thanalan resident excited about the prospect of owning her own home, sends you on a quest to learn more about the auctions. You find out that only adventurers (a.k.a. player characters) can buy open plots of land in The Goblet. When you return to Imme to deliver the bad news, she says:

> "You've returned! Tell me, what have you learned of the auctions? Eh!? What do you mean it's reserved exclusively for adventurers? I mean sure, times are tough, and every nation is scrambling to attract formidable fighters... But what about my needs!? What about my forty acres and a chocobo? Bah, it's just not fair!"

With no statement after this one other than the game's "Quest Completed" message, the writer attaches discussions of reparations to Imme's bratty/entitled attitude, making the surprise racial context even more off-putting.

I'm hoping this was a localization issue; perhaps someone meant to say something like "What about the Ul'dahnian Dream?" and reference the all-too-unrealistic view of societal guarantees of homeownership and stability in the United States. But when I posted the issues on Twitter (and also reached out through PR channels), I was met with silence.

Cicero Holmes said on an episode of the Spawn on Me podcast,* "When someone says, 'I don't like the fact that this game is getting political,' that means, 'I don't like the fact that this game has gotten political *for me.*'" For many marginalized folks out there, we don't get to choose when a game "gets political"; our politics are thrust into the space when battered stereotypes surface. Immersion in the game world ceases when an issue connected to racial equality and justice simply flops down as casual conversation from a throwaway non-player character. Though I wouldn't say this quote "ruins" the game, it ruined it for me…I haven't been back to FFXIV since.

As a black game journalist, I feel like it's part of my job to discuss these facets of game culture and how they affect me. The gaming industry has made great strides over the past few years, but there are plenty more to take. When I call out these parts of game culture, even when I'm met with silence, it's in the hopes of making sure marginalized people aren't forgotten about in the game development process. I hope that I'll heard; I hope I'll help make space for games that create proud, strong representations of marginalized people of all kinds. And really, I hope that there'll be better hair styles available for black folks in character creators.

---

* Spawn on Me Episode 190—N-Word of a Rotten Racist Pie: https://www.youtube.com/watch?v=oGjaN9GO9Vs

CHAPTER 22

A Series of Half-Baked Ideas and Quarter-Assed Memes

Why I left Gaming Stories

Dorey T Shawn

I RECENTLY MADE A TEXT adventure game called *Sorting 63 Genders*, which was made in the textadventures.co.uk engine. *Sorting 63 Genders* was a mostly bad attempt at social commentary on a single tweet by U.S. Congressman Joe Walsh. The game I made attempted to poke fun at the flimsy idea of a truly binary world. My game let you "live the life of a boy or a girl," its core design ethos being to provide gameplay that emulates the friction one experiences in attempting to fit in in a world that holds the gender binary in higher regard than the happiness of individuals just trying to live their life.

But as I just said, the game was not very good.

Sorting 63 Genders could never be very good. Between my emotional state and the conditions of academia, I could never put my all into it. I desperately want to revisit and polish it. My experience of graduate school in North America has been the act of navigating power structures still stuck in a hegemony that prioritizes the ideas and advancement of white cisgender men while actively excluding the voices of queer or people of color. As a Master of Arts (MA) student, you are expected to fill your time with as much work as possible that will make your CV look attractive. You can only work for your department. You cannot work for more than ten hours a week. Graduate students are under constant stress about whether or not they can have supper next week. Sometimes, the things you want to work on the most wait in limbo for weeks as you wait for approval or feedback.

My interest in digital humanities was kick started by my social circles on the Internet intersecting with my reading of Marshall McLuhan's seminal text *Understanding Media*. I became obsessed with how people interface with technology. Specifically, I became incredibly enthralled over learning how different individuals interact with the trouble of representing one's self through the options of interaction provided by software and games, digital or otherwise. This has consumed and does consume my every waking moment. I'll be sitting in a park and see someone texting or playing *Angry Birds*, and I can't help but examine the implications of even that simple occurrence.

I never planned to go to graduate school. It was off my radar. After six years of stumbling between undergraduate programs, I was *tired*. Despite this, my undergraduate advisor managed to convince me that graduate school was the next step. I had no idea what I was going to do once I finished my undergraduate degree. I liked the idea of teaching a university class, though. After months of complex paperwork, and a ton of extra reading and writing outside my degree work, I was accepted into the University of Waterloo. I planned to do a master's and then a PhD there in order to eventually become a university professor. No one really talked to me about the lived reality of graduate school. Nobody warned me how intense and archaic the system really was.

So I went to grad school all doe-eyed and idealistic. I foolishly expected a utopia of fellow scholars who wanted to dig into media and use it as a sounding board for feminist critique. I wanted to take this theory and apply it to my meager game- and film-making skills. I wanted to create strong, decisive pieces of media that really challenged people's perceptions.

At best I feel like I have made some half-baked thoughts and quarter-assed memes.

I went into grad school expecting impostor syndrome. I expected to feel like I knew nothing and was incapable of learning. But I didn't expect to feel like academia was also incapable of learning from me.

I only recently realized I was nonbinary. My undergrad program was small—and feminist. Integrating my pronouns was quick and easy. In grad school, every decision to correct or not correct my pronouns in a class (as instructor or as a classmate) became a high-stakes bomb defusal with only seven seconds left on the clock.

I experienced an eternal power struggle between people seeing me as a white man and people seeing me as a queer threat. Being biracial and nonbinary, I didn't fit the mold of the typical academic. I constantly had to wonder if I should correct a classmate misgendering me when not directly in the conversation. "What if people accused me of using that as an ad hominem attack?" I would wonder. Do I ask my students to use Mx. Dorey and risk seeing my tenuous authority in the room crumble? This anxiety's texture feels uniquely different to the anxiety felt from being misgendered by strangers. The presumed kinship between instructor and student, or any two classmates in a graduate course, is at a much higher level of assumed intimacy than customer and client. When that intimacy is brought into question, at least for me, you can't help but think that you're making an already impossibly hard thing harder by simply existing.

Over the two years I spent earning my MA, I constantly struggled with how I might be making things worse just by being there. This was compounded by finally coming face to face with all of my anxiety over being half white and half Arab and being treated as both. Finally grappling with my life as a biracial Lebanese Arab because I finally was interacting with people visibly of color en masse as opposed to token members of New Brunswick's incredibly white population only intensified the trauma of graduate school. I am still not done examining what it meant to be the child of a person of color but have white privilege assumed because my skin is lighter than that of most Arabs.

Unless the course explicitly had feminist critique/social justice/representation in its title, every time I brought up the critique of a text on the basis of gender or racial sensitivity, the professor would deftly dodge my comment and shift the conversation elsewhere. Outside of "designated spaces," queer interpretations didn't matter here.

I'd also have the extreme "pleasure" of being stopped after class for a classmate to explain how they "respect me as a person and a scholar" but their opinion and what they know about "being a man in this world" has them disagree with my identity. I shook his hand after that and said thank you. But the real thing that was shaking was my heart and soul. I remember thinking, "What was even the point of that?" I stood there transfixed and overcome with dread. The power struggle was enough when you were butting heads with the established professors, but having my classmates treat me like an idea to "debate" was beyond heart wrenching.

Even my first time showing up to a feminist games circle felt problematic. I arrived first, because if I'm not ridiculously early, I'm dreadfully late. Every woman who wasn't an organizer side-eyed me constantly until I was introduced. After the introduction was fine, but thanks to my wide masculine frame and my tight budget, which makes shaving a luxury, people simply read me as a cis boy all the time.

I am leaving academia. Triple A studios are at the bottom of my potential job list.

Working close with middle state publisher First Person Scholar helped me keep an eye on the underbelly of both academia and the games industry and see the totality of their power structures. Certain other cultural movements have not helped my perception of either. It is a constant battle to reconcile my love for the medium with intense exclusion by authorities who study and play with it. There are only so many times you can be told your representation doesn't matter before you start to wonder if that is true.

Ultimately, both games and academia became clearly places that value cold-hearted "reason" over emotional considerations. I still want to and will make games, but I will be doing it on my own terms.

Academia is full of too many slow-moving approval processes and a poor regard for truly transformative works.

During the final meeting before I handed in the final project for the final class of my final year in school, I heard something that I cannot get out of my head. That meeting began with my instructor looking me dead in the eyes and saying, "they really hate us, don't they"? I remember gulping and averting my eyes downward, a slight blush tinting my cheeks. I really wanted to impress her with my work, so as she followed that up with, "I really think a project like yours is exactly what we need right now," my heart exploded in jubilation. Unfortunately, this was the only time I truly felt like my perspective as a biracial nonbinary human was truly valuable to the academy. Too little too late.

The games consumer market does not want the games I want to make. The enigma of crunch is just as bad as the pressures of academia. I need something else. Being hired would accuse any studio of "caving to PC pressures." I've barely done anything in this industry, and half the time I pass as a white male, but I'm already incredibly tired. So I will make games, slowly, in the margins of struggling to conform to the expectations of capitalism. I don't care if they hate us, and I don't care that I could not find a fit in academia; I'll try and make my games cool, exciting, and unique. But most importantly, I'll make them queer as I am. Somehow, I'll squeeze through these margins.

Index

Milton Keynes UK
Ingram Content Group UK Ltd.
UKHW031134141024
449569UK00006B/201